Alexander Gardiner Mercer

Christ and his teachings

Being the second volume of selections from the sermons of Alexander Gardiner Mercer

Alexander Gardiner Mercer

Christ and his teachings
Being the second volume of selections from the sermons of Alexander Gardiner Mercer

ISBN/EAN: 9783337264703

Printed in Europe, USA, Canada, Australia, Japan

Cover: Foto ©Lupo / pixelio.de

More available books at **www.hansebooks.com**

Christ and His Teachings.

BEING THE SECOND VOLUME OF SELECTIONS FROM THE

SERMONS

OF THE LATE

ALEXANDER GARDINER MERCER D.D.

NEW YORK:
ANSON D. F. RANDOLPH AND CO.
38 WEST TWENTY-THIRD STREET.
1889.

CONTENTS.

CHAPTER		PAGE
I.	I Know that my Redeemer Liveth	3
II.	Christmas	14
III.	Temptation of Christ	25
IV.	The Transfiguration	40
V.	The Lord's Supper	52
VI.	The Crucifixion	61
VII.	Easter	71
VIII.	The Ascension	80
IX.	Whitsunday	91
X.	The Exaltation of Christ	100
XI.	The Feast of Epiphany	106
XII.	The Character of Christ	117
XIII.	Who is the Son of Man?	124
XIV.	The Scribes and Pharisees	135
XV.	The Judgment	144
XVI.	The Exaltation of the Heart	155
XVII.	The Godlikeness of Man	168
XVIII.	The Deception of Sin	181
XIX.	The Obedient Son	193
XX.	Christ and the Gadarenes	204
XXI.	Man's Praise more than God's Praise	214

CHAPTER		PAGE
XXII.	THE GOOD SAMARITAN	223
XXIII.	WIDER VIEWS OF CHRISTIANITY	234
XXIV.	THE DEPTHS OF SATAN	248
XXV.	THE OFFICE OF JUDGMENT	255
XXVI.	GOD'S REBUKE OF APPEARANCES	265
XXVII.	THE SPIRIT OF CHRIST	275
XXVIII.	THEY REWARDED EVIL FOR GOOD	284
XXIX.	THE POWER OF WILL	292
XXX.	THE WISDOM OF GOD	
XXXI.	THE RIVER OF LIFE	
XXXII.	WORLDLINESS	

CHRIST AND HIS TEACHINGS.

I.

I KNOW THAT MY REDEEMER LIVETH.

For I know that my Redeemer liveth, and that he shall stand at the latter day upon the earth: and though after my skin worms destroy this body, yet in my flesh shall I see God: whom I shall see for myself, and mine eyes shall behold, and not another; though my reins be consumed within me. — JOB xix. 25-27.

THE Book of Job has been thought the oldest book in the world. Some scholars assign it to the time of Solomon; but, be that as it may, I believe it to have been a very ancient tale, coming from the land and time of Abram or his ancestors, or from countries lying in the same direction and from a people of the same race, holding the same pure elements of religion. I take it to be a poem or drama founded on a deep personal experience.

Job was an Arab chief, or emir, and like Abram seems not so much to have reached just and impressive ideas of God as to have inherited them. Abram and his children, the Hebrews, cleared, added to, and held firmly these ideas; but the ideas themselves date long before them, and to a distant region of the world.

Most singular to say, these races, holding such convictions as to God, seem yet to have taken no firm grasp on a future life. From this fact — namely, that they had some clear notions of God and his moral government, and yet were in darkness respecting a world beyond the grave — arose the greatest perplexity and even agony of their lives. God must be just; and yet look here at the strange injustice, and no other life to bring a remedy! But such was their confidence in God that they generally forced even this world into an appearance of justice. When, however, these conflicts rose so high as in this cruel personal experience of Job, who, conscious of uprightness, saw that he and all his were about to perish forever, what should he say?

According to his belief, when the righteous man was prosperous, then only was God acting justly and in character; or if a degree of severity was allowed to be intelligible and justifiable, it must be brief, and for some good end now and here. Yet in the face of this creed here was Job, a man without crime, bearing his faculties and fortunes meekly, yet everything going bitterly against him, and with every sign that it was about to end so.

What a horrible perplexity this man was in! His troubles mounted up to heaven; but the agony of his heart was greater than all. He must admit either that God was no true God, or that his consciousness as to his own rectitude was a delusion. In this condition

Job seems to me one of the most interesting sights ever witnessed. His bottomless grief touched even on despair and death; yet how affectionately he clung to God, at the same time never foregoing his deep conviction as to his own rectitude; on the one hand saying, "Though he slay me, yet will I trust in him," and on the other standing firm in his consciousness of right, and refusing to affect being a sinner, — refusing to lie unto God.

This was manly, and God approved it, at the same time teaching him that he carried it too far, — that he had "uttered that he understood not;" and thus he learned to "abhor himself and repent in dust and ashes." Yet God approved his sincerity. But there was another thing in him, — his faith in God.

Religious faith, in its most general sense, means the tenacious grasp of the heart on the right and good thing, especially upon its God, and committing one's self to God, whatever is against us, and at all hazards. It is, as Pascal says, "God sensible to the heart." It is "enduring, as seeing him who is invisible."

This feeling was almost unparalleled in Job, and I take the words of the text to be the grandest expression of faith ever uttered by mortal lips. "For I know that my Redeemer liveth, and that he shall stand at the latter day upon the earth: and though after my skin worms destroy this body, yet in my flesh shall I see God: whom I shall see for myself, and mine eyes shall behold, and not another; though my reins be consumed within me."

Some Christian people make mistakes about these words, which so beautifully describe Christ and the resurrection that they think Christ and the resurrection were consciously and definitely before the mind of Job. In substance they were implied, but in fact he meant consciously this: "My redeeming God will save me, and will do it even upon this earth, will do it even in this crumbling body, dying and virtually dead,— that is, will be just and merciful, even although it seems a stark impossibility."

Remember what it was to say this. He believed in his innocence, he believed God must favor the innocent in this life; yet he stood bereft of all outward good, his heart breaking, his wife turning from him, herself hopeless and scorning,— "Curse God, and die," — his friends upbraiding him, his loathsome body, eaten up with incurable disease (the leprosy), sinking into the grave,— he stood, I say, at such a moment, and, in a sort of defiance of all the facts of Nature, declared that an hour of redemption was coming to him, — yes, even to his body. "I know:" "I am sure that God is, that he is true, that even now behind the curtain he is there, that he feels, and is a Redeemer; and though utter destruction seems not only probable but actual, 'though worms destroy this body,' and though there be no proof or precedent or promise that all this shall or can be reversed" (he stood so early in the world that he knew nothing to sustain him), "yet I know it will be reversed, and, 'though my reins be consumed within me,' I know that I shall at last see the Redeemer, — with these my eyes see him. Yes, and I shall be clothed again with my flesh, though that flesh be now crumbling before the worm."

He had in reality such a confidence in the perfection of God his Redeemer, that he knew he would bring a redemption corresponding to the worst exigency, whatever it might be; and so I say that this really preached a principle which contained all possible deliverances, and of course that of Christ and the resurrection. The principle is that whatever is demanded of the justice and becoming to the mercy of God shall take place in body as well as soul. If you had asked Job, "Do you expect that God will come forth as a man, or in some grander material form, and stand upon the earth, his brightness darkening the sun?" — if you had asked him, "Do you expect that your body will actually die and go to dust, and that then a resurrection of justice shall take place?" — he would, I think, have answered: "I know not how, or when, or in what way; I only know that God lives, and is not dead, and that he is the Redeemer of his children; I only know that, standing back now, he will stand forward, that impossible things will be possible, and that, though all Nature were condensed into one barrier of iron to stop him, he will go through it to save me, — nay, that in this very scene of sorrow, and in this very body of death, he will make life and joy to live, that eye to eye I shall behold him, even I, a dying worm." Thus he soared he knew not whither, like the hooded falcon, all darkened, but still ascending towards the sun.

I call that the sublimest thing a human being ever did. Now, how unspeakably has God vindicated this confidence! The Book of Job closes with the spectacle of one redemption, a personal redemption, one vindication. But the real and great, the universal redemption, of which this personal redemption of Job was but the shadow and symbol, has also in due time dawned; and how sublime that vindication! Job's confidence in God's triumphant mercy to soul and body hinted in substance of Christ and the resurrection; but the great truth was, in fact, as a scroll rolled up. It was reserved for us to see it unrolled. In these latter days the Redeemer *has* stood upon the earth,—a Redeemer indeed! The salvation of body and soul, which was but a poor, brief thing in Job's best apprehension of it, we see to be the eternal regeneration of one and the eternal resurrection of the other; and we now know, in a sense unspeakably exalted, that, though worms destroy this body, and though our reins be consumed within us, yet in our flesh shall we see God.

This view of the words of Job leads me to believe that not only in this case, but in all cases, now as well as then, every moral prediction of the heart, however impossible the event seems, will also surely be realized. But observe, I say *moral.* There are many desires, the strongest in the human breast, innocent wishes, — for example, family wishes for a domestic heaven, — which may be realized, but of that we have no assurance. But the deep demands of the moral heart are, I believe, certain to be fulfilled. To be sure, as to time and manner, our presumptuous ideas will be disappointed. Many people, for example, if they have a just quarrel, personal, national, or of a church, look that all matters shall be shortly set right, forgetting that the just Judge has his own way and his own great times. Why, generations and hundreds of generations have not yet lifted from the earth some of the sorest evils it groans under: "How long, O Lord, holy and true, dost thou not judge and avenge our blood on them that dwell on the earth?" But do not on this account, as some weak people do, finding that the Lord delayeth his coming, begin to doubt whether there is any right, and in effect blaspheme God and turn away from him.

"Careless seems the great Avenger; . . .
Truth forever on the scaffold, Wrong forever on the throne, —
Yet that scaffold sways the future, and, behind the dim unknown,
Standeth God within the shadow, keeping watch above his own."

Why judge his slowness or his inscrutable methods? Of one thing can we be sure, — that the deep and sacred demands of our hearts, our consciences, are the same as God's wishes, and that his wishes must one day stand forth as facts.

This is faith; and to know it is living faith; and of what value, of what power, is it! To dare to believe that which is thought impossible, to push aside the wisdom of the prudent, and to become in effect a fool, to trust and act with utter disregard of all evidence but the evidence of an enlightened heart,— that is the divine spark in man, and has wrought all the spiritual wonders in history. See here in this case this outburst of Job's confidence in his Redeemer,— perhaps the most magnificent words spoken in history, and of sublime effect.

I now ask, What is *our* creed? Have *we* a living God, a Redeemer? Can we say, "I know that my Redeemer liveth"? The contrast seems shameful; but I must not overstate it. If Job had stood firm in the exaltation of that moment, then indeed the contrast would be overwhelming, and we might despair. But that was far from the case, and this fact might as well be confessed; I think the infirmities of good men one of our greatest aids, for they save us from despair.

One or two great things the heart of Job never let go,— his consciousness of his own sincerity and his affectionate cry after God; but everything else wavered. The same man who uttered the sentence of the text, almost in the same breath, in this very chapter, says: "God hath overthrown me, and hath compassed me with his net. Behold, I cry out of wrong, but I am not heard: I cry aloud, but there is no judgment." And so in a hundred other places. It is not just, then, to rate ourselves by the highest feeling of Job; but have we that which he never lost? And have we ever a moment when with our whole hearts and with uplifted hands we can claim that we have a Redeemer and that we know it, — when we can look upon the grave and yet know that none are dead, — a moment when we are sure that God shall root out not only all oppression from the earth, but all wrong and sin from our own hearts, — that his hand shall find out the weeds of the world, as the hand of the husbandman finds the weeds of the field? Do we ever know this? Oh the vast difference between those men who can only say, "I have heard a rumor from the Lord," and those who have "seen him with the seeing of the eye"!

The coming of Christ is a reality. Whether he will stand as a visible figure upon the earth, or whether his coming will be, as many of his past comings have been, in spirit and in power, I do not know. But come he must, and in such eminence that "every eye shall see him." This will be to the whole world. To each man, of course, the same thing essentially will take place in a few days or months: I mean at his death, when he passes forth into the presence of his Judge. Whether in that Judge he will find also a Redeemer will depend on the fact whether the heart realizes and trusts in him.

Is this our Redeemer a reality to us? If our lives are smooth and prosperous, I fear not. If we have been tried like Job, then possibly we believe like him. Usually the invisible is like the heaven of stars in the daylight; but when God makes the daylight of the world darkness, then heaven comes forth. And usually this will not be done by ordinary griefs, for these make the hold on the world tighter; and I believe that many people never know more than these, and go through life without feeling that sort of trouble which sweeps everything from beneath the feet. When that comes, when the spirit dies in the breast, when we feel that inexpressible divorce between us and all, the agony of utter loneliness and hopelessness, then we are in a manner forced upon a Redeemer; we pour out our tears unto God; we stretch forth our hands towards him, if so be there may be hope.

Infinitely precious, then, are our troubles,—infinitely precious is death,—which constrain us to reach out for some one to redeem from trouble and sin and the grave. He slays us, that we may trust in him.

Unnumbered generations in Christian lands have been carried to their rest under the sound of these sublime words. They meet the dead as they are brought into our churches; they make the dead to speak, saying, "I know that my Redeemer liveth;" they make the living who survive, respond to the utterance of the solemn and touching consolation, saying, "Yes, we know that our Redeemer liveth." So over each of us, even of us, and of the children, over us and as if from us and for us, the same voice will be heard.

Will it announce the truth? In our flesh shall we see God? Yes, if we have indeed lived in this faith. How then will the way to the tomb be illuminated! What an indescribable halo of comfort and peace will rest upon the senseless clay!

II.

CHRISTMAS.

Let us now go even unto Bethlehem, and see this thing which is come to pass.—LUKE ii. 15.

SO said the shepherds one to another. The great sight of the universe was at Bethlehem on that day; and thence afterward forever, when men, or creatures above men, would seek the most wonderful, they make their pilgrimage back to that point. So, once more, let *us* go now even unto Bethlehem, and see this thing which is come to pass.

The sight was a new-born babe. Look simply at that. Coming in and away from all the regions of wonder which surround Christ, omitting all the wonder that concerned him through the Jewish history, through the whole story of men, or all that far higher story of those inconceivable facts and preparatory eras which, "or ever the earth was," moved forward to this issue; omitting the wonder of this Being as he became known, standing in the midst of us a living man, and all that scene of grace and truth and suffering; omitting whatever has followed from him (that Great Cause thrust into time and the world), whatever has come from him up to this moment, and all that must come in the periods yet before us, — omit whatever you can omit, and the greatest of the wonders remains, — a new-born child sent out from God. Let us now go to Bethlehem and see this one innocent sight.

For this birth was "the Word made flesh." Among all the births of God, the births of suns or sun-like spirits, this birth, which had eternally promised itself, now came forward in its order, a thing that had "come to pass."

Behold it! Stop and look well at it! It is the great fact in the history of the universe, and the great fact, if the language be allowed me. in the history of God. One thing is certain: either the birth of the Divine in the form of a babe is an incredible folly, or the most awful and delightful of facts; and that man, advanced as far as he is, does for the most part, and in the face of all the difficulties, believe that fact, is either the greatest scandal or the greatest glory of the human race. But whether he believes or disbelieves, even by these contradictions the wonder and the interest of the event are enlarged.

Speak not of any other history, — of the whole crowd of events behind us. They are as nothing. Speak not even of the truly grand world of truth, which the light of the human eye has illumined for us on every hand. The whole blaze of fact and truth together fades and looks like the light of a candle when the morning sun has come in.

God with us, — made flesh and dwelling among us! It strikes all as something of unspeakable strangeness; but it is both necessary and fit that it should appear so. Necessary, for at every step we descend into the deeps of God; his nature and ways must rise up before us with an eternal strangeness about them. And is it not fit as well as necessary? Is not pure wonder a right state of the finite spirit as it stands before the Infinite? And is it not the source whence come blended adoration for the awful greatness which passes out of our conceptions, and that sublimity of trust, even in the fearful and uncertain darkness, which emotions lie at the base of all religion forever, the very foundation ties connecting together God and the creature? Indeed, to excite wonder, unspeakable wonder, is always the study — I might almost say the artifice — of the Divine Spirit as it moves working in the world around us; for it is providing thus for all the conscious universe the instigation which lifts the forehead in eager aspiring, and bows it in awe, and thus bows it and lifts it forever; with an eternal wish forever lifts it, with an eternal awe forever sinks it, — which makes the worship of spirits, be they men or high as gods.

The strangeness of this spectacle, then, which angels may bend over, does not deter me. But I must say that the man learned in the history and tendencies of human nature sees here what looks at first as one instance (though it may be he will allow the purest) of that idolatrous bent of the heart which must have whatever it thinks divine embodied. He forgets, however, that this powerful bent, and I may say necessity, of human nature to realize God only under sensible forms made it probable that a true manifestation of God would be accommodated to that very need.

The best manifestation of God is no abstract thing; it is that which gives a pure display of God's nature in the form which best takes hold of man's nature as it is, — that is, which best combines purity with power. And has this not been well done? Is there any possibility within the range of wise thought that it could have been differently or better done than when "God sent forth his Son, made of a woman"?

Conceive a man who really feels and knows that in this human form is the very Son of the Highest; he will feel all through him such an influence as the idea of God invisible never has given and never could give him; and this simply because of the union of spirit with sense impressing a being who is himself sense and spirit, and who cannot, do as he may, rise entirely above himself. But when you add to the mere power given by this union of the divine with the material the means it affords for bringing out the unknown feelings of the Divine Heart, for showing God to be what by any other means than God embodied — God suffering — could never have been made known, — I say this, distinctly conceived, gives not only irresistible power to old truth, but pours out a startling revelation of light from the centre of the Soul of God, which will, like the tide of an ocean, sway back the spirits to their source and home.

I stand then over the cradle of Christ to-day, with joy not only that here is my Saviour, but that this is he who leads me back to God, who teaches me best what God is, and even through that body of flesh and bones and nerves and senses, even through that, leads me into the hidden secrets of the Divine Heart.

Did I not speak truth, then, when I said that from all points and places of the future all spirits of whatever height will forever revert to this point and place, and the words of the shepherds be the worlds of all races in all worlds and in all heavens, "Let us now go even unto Bethlehem, and see this thing which is come to pass"?

But the sight is not ended with the fact of the incarnation of the Divine Word. There was a divineness in the way in which it was done. Study it for a moment. "When he bringeth in the first-begotten into the world," it is a matter of the most curious interest how He will do it.

Hear, then, once more the narrative: "And so it was, that while they were there, the days were accomplished that Mary should be delivered. And she brought forth her first-born son, and wrapped him in swaddling-clothes, and laid him in a manger; because there was no room for them in the inn. And there were in the same country shepherds abiding in the field, keeping watch over their flock by night. And lo, the angel of the Lord came upon them, and the glory of the Lord shone round about them; and they were sore afraid. And the angel said unto them, Fear not; for behold, I bring you good tidings of great joy, which shall be to all people. For unto you is born this day, in the city of David, a Saviour, which is Christ the Lord. And this shall be a sign unto you; Ye shall find the babe wrapped in swaddling-clothes, lying in a manger. And suddenly there was with the angel a multitude of the heavenly host praising God, and saying, Glory to God in the highest, and on earth peace, good will toward men."

Now, this seems to me a grand epical and a sweet pastoral history; for it is surrounded by sounds as of shepherds' bells mingling with the voices of angels and spirits, and by sights uniting the simplicity and innocency of the earth with the regality of the heavens.

The first thing to which I ask attention here is the style of the supernatural. Had it been left to man to introduce a God, either the manifestation would have been wild and grotesque, or the chief traits, even with the most refined, would have been those of power and exterior magnificence, for these are the things most divine to man. The blending also of the human with the divine would have been awkward and inharmonious, or this would have been avoided only by sacrificing the one to the other; and no doubt, even if it had been the manifestation of an inferior deity, the human part would have been sacrificed to the divine, and a lurid light of prodigy would have shone over the whole, — a " light that never was, on sea or land." Instead of all which we find that though this divine story of Christ came from the bosom of the people, even from the Jews of that day, there is nothing grotesque, nothing of mere prodigy here.

We, whose taste in the wonderful has been formed and refined and sobered under the Christian ideal of it, can hardly estimate, unless by taking our stand in the mythologies of other religions, or even in the best conceptions of the supernatural found in the poetry or philosophy of the world, the marvellous elevation and refinement of this narrative. We do not know, unless by an observation and consciousness of our nature the widest and deepest, how late and how difficult a thing it is to touch the supernatural world with dignity. Whoever approaches that mighty sphere seems to suffer some belittling or derangement of faculty.

So also as to the amount of it. Instead of being lavished, as is nearly inevitable where the whole range of the possible is put within our reach, there is here and elsewhere through the life of Christ a striking economy of the supernatural. There seems just as little of it as the circumstances would allow.

Observe here the blending of the natural and the supernatural. The human aspect is kept entirely human, the divine is left entirely divine, and neither overshadows the other. Nor is there an attempt to force the human into a consistency with the divine. I mean that there is no endeavor to make this human child Jesus equal to his awful character, — to give to the babe such an air as would harmonize it with the surrounding of heavenly songs and angels and the star and the magi; there is not even a halo of divine light about the head; he is not depicted as strangling serpents in his cradle. There is the babe, and not anything but a helpless human babe.

This was the most original and bold of conceptions, and it does not seem to have been sufficiently observed. None of the wonder or the greatness is in the child, but around it and above it. How new! how unlike all things else in the history of mere wonder! What immense extremes are here brought together without the least gradation of one to the other! So unlike man! Yet is this, if it be examined, infinitely graceful, touching, and significant, and sheds, as was intended, divine honor upon our nature as it is, upon womanhood, upon childhood, associating together, as if it were a natural thing, the fairest and highest things of heaven with the simple and humble innocency of a babe. See all the powers of God surrounding it, but not touching it, not raising it to honor it, but honoring it in its simple helplessness! Was ever a sight more impressive to the imagination? But its significance is beyond its picturesque effect. For here begins that history of a Being who, while called the Son of God, and bearing in his hand the powers of the world unseen, could not, would not, do anything for himself; but who, from the babe wrapped in swaddling-clothes by Mary his mother, to the helpless figure lifted and fastened to the cross, "was made in all things like unto us."

Notice further that the conception here of the true dignity of God is something quite startling. Power and exterior magnificence there were, to be sure, sufficient to illustrate and bear witness of his birth, but observe of how peculiar and subdued a tone were even these. There were blessed beings filling the midnight heavens, not with startling exhibitions of power, but only singing in the ears of simple shepherds a cradle-hymn sweetly blending with the image of the Virgin's child and his reign of holy innocence, and all unlike the regal grandeur of earthly imaginations; this too, quiet as it was, lasting but for a moment, and then the heavens shut, — shut until his coming again, — and the child committed first to a mother's bosom (the only home where the Son of man ever laid his head), but only there that he might be nourished to bear all human infirmities, and with them darkness and poverty and contumely and stripes and death. That is, when God wished to set forth the inmost brightness of his own nature, the express image of the Highest, he sought the lowest forms of humiliation to show it in. He dismisses heaven; he dismisses the white and blazing companies of angels so soon as they have announced him; he stops the only carol ever sung over him almost as soon as it has begun; he shuts out all the celestial. The Divine inhabits the body of a child. It is a child so born that the manger is the place for him,— there is no room in the inn. He lives a human life upon the earth, choosing the lowest and hardest fortunes, but through all thinking the highest, feeling the purest, working the noblest, and blending all together at last in the death of the cross. This, I say, is God's conception of how God might best live and show the godlike. Behold it! Ye ambitious for the splendors and power of the world; ye selfish, striving sons of men; ye who sacrifice the things within for the things without, to whom a blazoned name and rank, the shining of gold, and all the equipage of life outshine the pure, generous thought, outshine the quiet humble spirit, the daily and obscure self-denial, outshine the life which, though poor and dark without, is lighted within with the glory of God and of the Lamb, — all ye, see! be rebuked! be shamed! Learn ye to-day the kingly style, the Christian rank; for on this day, by and through this birth, God meant to reverse the whole prejudices of the race,— prejudices which have sunk through and through and saturated the heart, the imagination, and the very ground of the soul. He meant this as a costly overthrow of the taste, of the wisdom, of the vain admirations, of the whole established ideal of human beings.

But is it overthrown? The style of the king rules the heart of the people and shapes their lives; but the style of this our King, what heart adores it, what life is moulded to it? Ah, if he were our King, his ways, his fashion — may I call it? — would seize our hearts. A little way, indeed, it has penetrated. The whole world should bow down and thank God to-day that a new taste, from the moment of that birth, began gradually to dawn. I own it with joy, that the birth of the child Jesus has not been in vain. I own what he has already done in rectifying the false estimates of men, in penetrating through blood, tradition, pomp, to set our hearts upon the value of the spirit, and to teach us to measure ourselves and others by the measures of the soul.

Let us with the eager hearts of those shepherds revisit in mind that village of Bethlehem, and gaze long and thoughtfully at the sight which is there come to pass. He blasphemes this day who does not remember Christ with love and adoring awe, with shame for meanness and sorrow for sin, with wishes, and the beginnings of tender hopes. If nothing of this is yours, then the birth of this Saviour is nothing to you. He may have taught in your streets, and eaten and drunk in your presence, but verily I say unto you, he knows you not.

III.

TEMPTATION OF CHRIST.

Then was Jesus led up of the Spirit into the wilderness to be tempted of the devil. And when he had fasted forty days and forty nights, he was afterwards a hungered. And when the tempter came to him, he said, If thou be the Son of God, command that these stones be made bread. But he answered and said, It is written, Man shall not live by bread alone, but by every word that proceedeth out of the mouth of God. — MATT. iv. 1-4.

IN representing this wonderful transaction to ourselves we may without blame, I trust, and with profound reverence, do it in this way. The baptism being over which had publicly set Jesus apart to his great office of world-Redeemer, and new and mighty measures of the Spirit being accorded him, there became at once a necessity that the great temptation of his existence should be placed here, that thus the struggle might be carried into all the experience and call forth all the energies of his nature.

Perhaps through the whole of this record, or of all the records of man, there is not a more meaning story than this; and yet there is much mystery and difficulty about it. It is variously conceived. But I shall not enter upon a discussion as to whether it is to be taken literally, just as it stands, or whether the working of the spirit of evil in the mind of Christ with such unusual power as his unusual character and work would naturally call forth, aided by the long solitude, fasting, and weakness of body, did not make a mental experience represent itself to him as an outward transaction, just as is always in some degree found in the experience of men of mighty faith in the invisible, and called through mighty struggles to mighty works; or whether Christ in narrating it afterwards did not use a description or figure which to his hearers seemed literal; or, in fine, whether the narrators themselves intended it to be wholly literal, or in part figurative. This is a most difficult question to determine. Whatever view be taken of it, the spiritual meaning remains the same; and it is that only which I wish to interpret.

Conceive, then, the mind of Christ at this period. He had become conscious that he was the Messiah. Think of the solemn depth of excitement aroused by the circumstances of the baptism. Feeling then within an incredible access of Spirit, he was "led up of the Spirit into the wilderness."

We can conceive how this would naturally arise, for God does everything as near naturally as may be. A powerful, overmastering impulse was felt for seclusion and preparation. So he was swayed towards the wilderness, where for a long period the exalted spiritual condition he was in superseded the ordinary wants of the body, or enabled him to triumph over them. During this period of thought and plan the magnificence of the powers he felt to be in his possession, and the stress of his sympathy with the popular and universal idea and wish as to the Messiah, must have influenced his mind. When at length, however, in the multitude of his thoughts, growing gradually weaker in spirit and body, doubts of himself began to rise, proportioned in intensity by the greatness of the reaction, — in this condition the united motives of intense hunger and desire to resolve doubt solicited him to make bread in order to allay appetite and prove that he was the Son of God. This he resisted.

If a full consciousness of his nature and of the future had possessed him at all times, without weakness or doubt, then he could not have lived a human life of infirmity, temptation, and sorrow. Such a consciousness would have borne him over all, as a strong wind bears a cloud into the higher atmosphere and holds it there, in sight of the earth, but far out of reach of living sympathy and fellowship with its life.

Now I see in all this what I believe the Christian world overlooks too much in contemplating Christ, — namely, what his life and peculiar trials were. Taking any view of him we may see fit, there were struggles arising from the peculiarities of his relations which were perhaps his greatest. See what the temptation is made up of, and conceive the intensity of it: "If thou be the Son of God, command that these stones be made bread."

There was much to say for such a course. First,

for the relief of doubt. Can we conceive anything so apt to try him? We know that doubts of the Father's faithfulness to him were allowed to come in and flood his soul with darkness in the last hours of his human agony: "My God! my God! why hast thou forsaken me?" I have the impression that this temptation of doubt, the most terrible temptation, I think, which ever besets the sincere heart, was not through all his life wanting to him who was made in all things like unto us. Here at the beginning of his career as Messiah this doubt was likely to occur with the greatest force. Up to this time he had been living as any Jewish youth, with a growing consciousness, no doubt, of his peculiar relation to his Father, shown strikingly when at twelve years of age he left Joseph and Mary, to be, as he expressed it, about his Father's business; but this, I suppose, was a prominent and rare exhibition of this state of feeling, or it alone would not have been narrated. He grew, I dare say, through a life of beautiful but natural boyhood and early manhood, until the time came for his showing unto Israel. Then suddenly, at his baptism, he was publicly recognized by John, and by the descent of the Spirit seen by his eyes and felt inwardly by his heart. Under the force of this new revelation of himself to himself he was led up into the wilderness, and there, while yet unconfirmed in this startling, awful consciousness that he, even he, was the Messiah, he was subjected at once to such desertion, such bodily need (and nothing troubles an aspiring soul quicker than the wants of the animal nature), such an inroad of thoughts, doubts, wonderings, that a tempest seemed to shake the very foundations of his consciousness. Oh for light! give me light! The devilish darkness seemed to smother him; and then, just then, in this hunger of soul, the voice came, "If thou be the Son of God, command that these stones be made bread, — at once, by a word, satisfy your mind and feed your body; clear all mystery at once, by simply using the powers you have, to turn these stones to bread."

Now this was a temptation, to be sure. Why should not his divine power be used here? It was his, quite as much as the gifts of a gifted man are his, and infinitely more. The best of men would count it an incredible hardship if he were not allowed to use his talents for his own good or pleasure. He would say: "I am ready to own that the highest end of my gifts is the good of others and the honor of my Creator; but then, I am to love others as myself, and not more than myself, and so I may use my powers for my own sake also." If we consider the height of the gifts of Christ, and the lowliness and meekness of his position when stripped of them, we can have some thought what an habitual self-denial it was, never to use his powers for his own advantage.

Here, however, was a case clearly beyond even this. The question was, Would he use his gifts to clear doubt? — that first; but beyond that still, to avert death itself? "I perish with hunger," was his feeling. Could he do a wiser act than to save himself by a simple word? — for see what hung upon that life. Could he not employ one drop of his almighty deep of power to save himself? "But speak the word, and these stones at your feet will be bread, and body and soul will both go forward in the strength of this food."

See the stress and reasonableness of the tempter. So much motive would press, even were there no physical temptation! But the keen pangs of hunger came forward with all the forces of life bent with incredible craving for food, — an instinct of such ferocity as to bear down all the humanity before it, as even can make the mother devour her child, — a hunger for food, to which, together with the hunger for life, the Creator has committed the preservation of our being, and the blind, resistless strength of which survives and triumphs even over better instincts, and stands as the last and mighty warder of the sacred treasure of life!

Hunger! Not one out of millions of beings ever knows anything of it but its first whisper; its moans and cry are unknown even to the imagination. You may hear it, indeed, echoed and imaged in the howl of the beasts at midnight in the wilderness.

Here, then, was the temptation of the Son of God. Arrayed against his holy will was, first, the power of natural doubt that is in the heart, its weakness seeking assurance; second, the power of evil that is in the reason presenting a case in which the highest intelligence, unenlightened and unsupported by the noblest virtue, would have erred; and, third, the stress of the very inmost of the bodily powers, hunger, — the solicitations of the most refined self-regard through all the range of it, and masked under public motive, — the whole contest and force of the merely human soul, thought, body, centred in one against him; not against the centre of his virtue, but against the simplicity and entire purity of it.

This was the tempting. I suppose I have overstated nothing, for all this is implied here, and much more. And now, how was it met? "If thou be the Son of God, command that these stones be made bread. He answered and said, Man shall not live by bread alone, but by every word that proceedeth out of the mouth of God." "Command that these stones be made bread. Use your powers." "No; for that cause came I not into the world, but to obey as a son; and in doing this I know my truest life will live, and even my lower will not perish."

Observe, throughout these temptations, that they are all addressed to him as the Son of God, assuming that he should claim personal privileges on that account. On the other hand, he answers them all, assuming the rank of mere manhood, and refusing to use his divine powers for himself. "I am here as the Son of God in my powers toward men, but as a man only, and with all a man's needs and duties and feelings, in my relations to God." To maintain this position was necessary to his purposes, and constitutes, I think, one of the greatest trials, as well as one of the greatest wonders, of his career.

"No; for God has taught me that over, and even against the ordinary ways of nature, should it be necessary, his power will interfere for me if I trust in him. I am perishing with hunger, yet my life is not dependent on bread, but upon the will of God, who can give me manna in this desert, as once he did of old. Why then should I use the power of miracles merely to escape dependence upon God? for that moral life of manhood is a far higher work for me than to succor myself by miracles. He has placed me in a position of need to call forth my trust in him. I shall not make my miracles a means of getting clear of my trust, which is a higher act, infinitely, than the use of power. I must be made perfect through sufferings. So far from being distinguished by using power in my own behalf, I should forego power, and commit myself to God more than all others."

Here, then, he for the first time, and out of the depths of his heart, discerned the wonderful rule for the use of his supernatural powers. He was to make trust his help. Filial love and trust were all he had of power to meet all want, natural or supernatural. What force in this thought! "Man does not live by bread alone." "Show thyself Son of God," says the tempter, "by making bread of stones." "I show myself such," Christ replies, "by refusing to live through the trials of human life with any aids different from those common to all men, and by refusing to exert any power but the divine power of trust open to all."

We see in this a rule of judgment as to all his experiences. Wherever trial was concerned,—and was it not concerned in all?—we must conceive his experience as identical with our own; impossible perhaps in certain things, but heightened in others. "The Son of God will be a mighty power, serving himself," says the Devil. "The Son of God is a mighty trust, serving God," says Jesus. "The Son of God will save himself by physical power." "I live by trust," says Christ.

See how wonderfully opens that divine philosophy of faith afterwards taught to all, and constantly reiterated, but which he taught not as a mere rule out of his thought, but which he first lived, and taught to others out of his own heart! Here he began his public life by showing a divine example of this philosophy, the energy of which is illustrious to the invisible worlds, and only dimly perceived by us. For who can measure the force of the motives which went against all this? Who can measure the measure of that holy energy which saw and worked out the divine ideal of generous trust against the most splendid worldly ideal, and in the face of such solicitation from body, soul, and spirit?

The intensest power of the universe seemed first drawn into self, and then that self, with all the unimaginable might of its interests, he yielded; the existence — shall I say it? — of Almightiness itself he seemed ready to sacrifice rather than violate that one element of life, love, which thus seems to be the life — yes, and the power — of Godhead itself. I say here was the trial of God.

And with what powers did I say it was met? By that power given to us. Look! through all the thirst of his needs, and though power lay around him like an overflowing river reaching to his lips, he never touched a drop of it, nor cooled his parching tongue, but lived his life of awful glory merely as a man, and with the powers and faculties belonging even to the meanest. Divine image! example of supreme height, set forth for us!

Now the great lesson here for the human race, and for us, stated generally, is that all temptations are to be met by trust; that in situations where it is actually impossible to help ourselves, or where, as in the case of our Lord, it would be doing a wrong to help ourselves, — that is, in cases where we are in effect powerless, in cases where we are called to bear, and not to do, the will of God, in suffering now, or in the menace of its coming, — in such cases as these, where the instinct of happiness, or the instinct of life itself, would tempt us to murmurings, to bitterness, to struggling blindly against accident, or evil fortune, or whatever it is in which the will of God appears, or to the use of unlawful or questionable means to relieve ourselves, then we are to say, " My happiness, my life, are not in bread alone, are not dependent on the good thing I now seem perishing for, but 'by every word that proceedeth out of the mouth of God' shall man live. My life rests directly and entirely on his word, and I am not made the dependent slave of the events or facts or laws of this world. His word spake into being the power of bread to nourish me, and of all natural good to please me, and it now can speak again and feed me anew on something else, providentially by changing my situation or changing my tastes; or, if it be necessary, miraculously; and if this should not take place, why, then I live still. How? Upon his will. It is his will that my body perish, but that my being shall live in a higher sense; that as the body flourished and grew, so the blood of my soul should grow vital, and the whole life of my soul expand, feeding in trust upon God himself; and so I rise superior to all ruin, and by means of ruin, living, when I perish, ' by every word that proceedeth out of the mouth of God.' "

There is something here to meet the very deepest experiences of our life. Once, many times, in our momentous human story, we too are in wilderness and seem to perish of hunger. Earnest, deep wants of our hearts, that will not hear of disappointment, are yet disappointed, and we perish. Through the wilderness, indeed, we go all our days, from the first. Everywhere, in everything, there is a check to our wishes. Through all the facts of life runs a will without us, which is against ours, and resists us and breaks us down at every turn. I mean that from the first cry of the infant, through all the wild outcries of our spirits, suppressed, but all the wilder, deeper, for that, the one fact is proclaimed, that the human being hungers in the wilderness, and like the beasts in this night of nature cries aloud for food unto God.

But if this cry of want is deep and piercing for what we have not, oh, how deeper, how inexpressible, when, having got, the heart is bereaved of its objects! We are beings who hunger for that which is not yet, and wail for that which was but is not now; and these tears, cries of man's hunger, go up constantly before God. What does it mean? Can we not understand, can we not master it? The Head of the race is Christ; and if we would catch the meanings of his life we could understand it, and if we would catch the spirit which he had, we could master it. In the Son of man in the desert, without food, behold yourselves! Satisfied as we may become at any moment, our natural life as a whole is — and is the most deeply felt to be by the deepest spirits — a hunger. Man is placed there, too, not by blind chance, but is "led up of the Spirit into the wilderness." Behold in this ourselves. This is not all confusion and meaningless: the Spirit has led us up into this life for great objects, — this, namely, by trial to bring out the vast spiritual powers which are possible to us, and which are eternal. These are, it seems, conditions of the birth of an immortal; and this our mortal life is but the soil and air out of which the plant is called to come and eternally to be. It is for the bringing forth of the true immortal man that all the appointments of this natural life, and all its costly sorrows, are not a superfluous and lavish waste of means and a more cruel waste of feeling, but a necessary, and, so far as may be, a merciful and economical preparative. "The creature was made subject to vanity, not willingly, but by reason of him who hath subjected the same in hope."

Being, then, led up to this life by the Spirit, to be tempted or tried, our one concern here is to know how to meet it so that these purposes be not frustrated; for if that be, oh, the waste of the very blood in our veins and the marrow in our bones, — waste of the throbs and agonies and life of our hearts; and then the waste of the spirit itself in the pure hereafter! With all the energy of attention and wish, then, look to what Christ did.

"Satisfy your hunger," says the tempter, "by any means in your power; let your first aim be to appease the cravings of natural life. Even if you have divine powers, prostitute them to this, and command that these stones be made bread."

This advice prevails; and see, the whole world follows it. Of all the hungry, how many reflect and say, "Why am I hungry; and has not my Father food enough and to spare, and shall I not return and look to him?" See the world all hungry, yet all seeking bread out of stones, some by begging, others by trying to command it, according to their characters and gifts.

But see Christ, the divine sufferer, the divine conqueror (and all not for his sake, but for ours); look at him! Who hungered like him? Yet he kept himself in his integrity. He reserved his high power for other purposes, and used the worst exigencies of his natural life to raise himself to a nearer trust in God. Go ye and do likewise. If you will forget for what you were sent into the world, and let the bitterness of disappointment harden your heart, or the sweet insinuations of temptation melt it, and persuade you that if you become but a little less pure or honest you can have your wish, — believe not that you will ever reach it. The soul cannot satiate its real hunger anywhere below itself. The stones will never become true bread, do with them what you will.

There are those who, when they find their worldly wishes hard to realize, lose in the strength of their hunger their scruples as to the means of satisfying it. Do you, in pursuit of any darling object, allow a little strain upon your conscience? Are you less open, less just, less merciful, less pure, that you may reach it? Or does it, at least, absorb all the finer faculties of your nature in its pursuit? Then you have not learned Christ so well as you ought.

Oh that we might all know it in the centre of us, — that man does not " live by bread alone, but by every word that proceedeth out of the mouth of God," — that in bereavements, or in the vast denial of our wishes, found in every bosom, we would learn to draw very near, and still nearer, to the source of true life, and trust there with all our souls, and gather life from that, though we be alone in a wilderness, and though we have no bread but the stones at our feet! "Seek ye first the kingdom of God, and his righteousness, and all these things shall be added unto you."

IV.

THE TRANSFIGURATION.

And it came to pass, about an eight days after these sayings, he took Peter, and John, and James, and went up into a mountain to pray. And as he prayed, the fashion of his countenance was altered, and his raiment was white and glistering. And behold, there talked with him two men, which were Moses and Elias: Who appeared in glory, and spake of his decease, which he should accomplish at Jerusalem. But Peter and they that were with him were heavy with sleep: and when they were awake, they saw his glory, and the two men that stood with him. And it came to pass, as they departed from him, Peter said unto Jesus, Master, it is good for us to be here: and let us make three tabernacles; one for thee, and one for Moses, and one for Elias: not knowing what he said. While he thus spake, there came a cloud and overshadowed them: and they feared as they entered into the cloud. And there came a voice out of the cloud, saying, This is my beloved Son: hear him. And when the voice was past, Jesus was found alone. And they kept it close, and told no man in those days any of those things which they had seen. — LUKE ix. 28–36.

THIS is one of the most singular, attractive, and grand, of all the records of this wonderful Book. The scene was formerly supposed to be Mt. Tabor, the highest peak in Galilee. At all events, it was "a high mountain." He took by selection three of his disciples into this lofty, removed spot, where there was peculiar solitude; where they were, as Saint Mark says, "apart by themselves."

Now, as to the actual order of the events there is some confusion in the various accounts, but they probably took place as follows: There, while he prayed he was transfigured; and Moses and Elias were with him. "But Peter and the other two disciples were heavy with sleep." I suppose that here, as in the scene in Gethsemane, while their Lord was engaged, they slept; and so the transfiguration and the high conference took place, and had continued, how long we know not. But they awoke. "And when they were awake, they saw his glory, and the two men that stood with him."

Now, this seems but a splendid dream, a divine pageant rising in the sleeping visions of some holy soul. It is, in fact, called a "vision," and there is something about it to tempt us to the impression that it is but a grandly mythical scene. So far, however, as the word "vision" goes, nothing visionary is implied. Its real use is, a transcendent sight. It may be spectral, but real. The scene opened, may stand out of local habitation in time or space, as in the vision of Saint Paul: "Whether in the body, or out of the body, I cannot tell;" but even then, the thing is none the less real.

If the object of the transfiguration was to introduce once and for a little while a divine glory into the natural and homely life of Christ on earth, it could not be done better; the style of the supernatural is utterly free from the various traits of human origin which always accompany the false supernatural. The scene is simple, significant, divinely grand, and without exaggeration or excess. If it seems, from its peculiarity and splendor and exaltation, as contrasted with the extreme realness and homely plainness of the ordinary history, surprising and like fiction, consider that this could not have been otherwise. To introduce a momentary effulgence into the life of Christ, for which there were most important purposes, must have conveyed the impression of magnificent fiction and dream. Try your conceptions upon it. Consider, besides, where this narrative is found, — in what Book, I mean, — and consider what Person it concerns, for what purposes. The parts of this sacred history of the Lord Jesus Christ are entitled to be judged together; and if so, it is most important that in interpreting any part we remember the whole. Bearing in mind who Christ was, keeping in view the reasons for self-obscuration and humility in general, and on the supposition of the reality of spiritual life, which our senses darken as a veil, and make us absurdly sceptical of, — when we remember how a painter or sculptor who has the genius of his art may take the lowest and most earthly face, and, preserving a certain identity, may remould, relight, remodulate, so as to exalt it to an ideal grace and majesty, — we can have some conception of the change. "He was transfigured before them."

What, now, were the purposes of this scene? Two, chiefly, I suppose, — a purpose in respect to Christ, and a purpose in respect to these three witnesses and through them to the world.

First, a purpose in respect to Christ. Because of his divineness we forget that he was human. As in Gethsemane "there appeared an angel unto him from heaven, strengthening him," so here, — confirmed by the fact that the glory began, and perhaps was almost finished, before seen. And so, as if for a moment, the Father took him up into his original dignity, that he might go down again with increased power into the world.

But more obviously the effect of the scene was designed for others, to manifest forth his glory, that his disciples might believe on him. They needed it. About a week before, the melancholy future had been laid open to them. So he stood before them in his glory, transfigured so magnificently that only their indefinable sense of sameness preserved identity. The countenance and form which were "marred more than any man" were altered; the face became (ἕτερον) another, raised to such beauty and dignity as would allow one of these sober writers to say that it should be compared with the sun, — "and his face did shine as the sun," — and his very garments of such purity and splendor that the words used, bring before us the peculiar clearness of pure water, or the polish of a golden shield when it blazes in the sun, or the twinkling of a star and the flash of lightning.

For one moment "the King is seen in his beauty,"

seen as a figure fit to introduce pure life and immortality, — for one moment, to indulge a little a being who judges after the sight of his eyes. And not merely that his splendor was designed to impress, but the whole transaction to teach them — the celestial company — the relation in which he was here placed to those figures from the past, as one not divided from the past, or coming to destroy it, but to fulfil; to show that the past kingdom and the future were not two things but one thing.

And observe, from out of the past the two figures most significant were selected, — Moses, the establisher and lawgiver of the first kingdom; Elijah, its restorer, representing with Moses the whole company of the prophets. These " appeared in glory " with him. Two figures, glorious themselves and standing in the same atmosphere of glory with him, were a sort of symbolical method by which God owned, and as if enshrined, the past dispensations as his own. That was an important teaching then, and always. But there was another more important, — that these past dispensations should be seen by the Jews, but not too glaringly seen, vaguely seen, to be merged or lost in him. How is this indicated? Here is the difficulty; for this, the most needed, is the most vague.

The figures, to be sure, are in harmony; that is something. They are all lustrous, the past as well as the present; that is something more. But what informs us who of them are the servants and which the Son? Well, three things.

The first and slightest is this: that to these Jewish minds filled with unspeakable awe for Moses and the prophets both these figures are represented as subordinate throughout in small things, such as the order in which they are named. That they stand as mere preparers, though splendid, to the mysterious third and last One, who was the "author and finisher," is beautifully seen in this. Attend to the narrative: After the disciples had been roused from sleep, and had seen the Lord and the two who were with him, then it seems these two figures of the past began to recede. " And it came to pass, as they departed," or while they were departing, Peter, transported with their presence, cried out as if to detain them, " Master, it is good for us to be here: let these remain, and let us build three dwellings; one for thee, and one for Moses, and one for Elias." He wist not what he said, but in the wild joy of his heart he spoke out what he felt. But mark: "While he thus spake, there came a cloud and overshadowed them: and they feared as they entered into the cloud." It was the presence of the invisible God. "And there came a voice out of the cloud, saying, This is my beloved Son: hear him."

There, it seems to me, is the emphasis of the whole narrative. Let the shadows of departed systems depart; detain them not; build not for them; build no tabernacles for Moses and Elias; turn from them and from all other names. This is my beloved Son: hear him.

And, last of all, these great figures are presented as looking forward to his death. They "spake of his decease which he should accomplish at Jerusalem." This seems to intimate that all God had done before, in the Mosaic and prophetic economies, yet looked forward and pointed to a coming *death*, as the object of attention, — the death of Christ. They "spake of his decease which he should accomplish at Jerusalem," or rather they spake of his "exodus," departure, or, according to the old use, a departing and leading out of bondage, — this word seeming to say that his death was that final and universal redemption from bondage which was rehearsed, foreshadowed, by the great symbol of the exodus of Moses and the people from the foreign bonds and taskmasters of Egypt into the land of liberty and rest. But as that exodus was of the earth, this heavenly, so this Deliverer also was spiritual and heavenly and hence above all, to whom of necessity Moses and Moses' work was a small and carnal thing, and but for a moment.

If this decease was the great event of interest to these glorious persons, it could only have been because of its spiritual effect upon the world; and as it was a death to be accomplished, and accomplished at Jerusalem, the Mount of Expiation, and accomplished by an exalted Being, in a mighty suffering, for spiritual purposes, it was of course in a real sense a sacrifice; and a sacrifice of such substance, of such sort, of such magnitude, that all others became at once mere gross shadows, so spiritualizing, so divinely enlarging the very idea of sacrifice, as of course to terminate and put away and put to shame all other sacrifices, except as mere figures of the true. The temple and altar and sacrifices of Moses, all founded on the idea of death for sin, all necessarily become nothing, and all must disappear, when we see Moses himself speaking of the Lord's death, speaking of such another death than that he had appointed, such other blood from that he had poured out.

So when Moses, the great institutor of the altar and the victim, spoke of His death, when he who appointed the lamb of the atonement saw before him another Lamb of sacrifice, as it is evident he did, — it is not straining the matter too far to think that it was intended to intimate that the old priest who offered the blood of bulls and goats, and the old animal victims themselves which were offered, became nothing, and he who instituted them nothing, and that the whole system was at once fulfilled and lost in a Being who came bringing a divine humanity as an offering to God and man.

So much, then, as to the significance of this scene in reference to the sacrificial side of the old economy represented by Moses, and then as to the line of prophets whom Elias stood for. They were essentially spiritual teachers; in what sense, then, could they look forward to his death as fulfilling and merging their function in a higher? I answer that that death, both for light and power, both for instruction and effect upon the human soul, consummated all teaching. The blood of the cross was a voice crying out of the ground, and shaking not the earth only, but also the heavens. What was the whole crowd of prophets to that one Prophet perishing for the race? Was their object deliverance, redemption, to deliver the people from all thraldom without and within, from the bands of folly and crime and sense? Was this the end of their sublime agonies? If so, can you conceive anything finer than that this goodly fellowship of the prophets should look forward with unspeakable solemnity and interest to that death which should ring "freedom" and "redemption" into every ear through all the coasts of the earth? The old law, the old holiness and justice, breathed through their lips, was weak when they cried the loudest, the ear was heavy that it could not hear; but here was a death to be "accomplished," which should awe the world; a death which was itself obedience to all law, honor to all justice at any cost, and the promulgation of the new and higher edicts of mercy to mankind. How full, then, of meaning that these sublime figures, speaking for law, for sacrifice, for spiritual life, should appear with him in glory, themselves glorious, and yet speaking of and looking to that death!

This subject will have enough of practical instruction and impressiveness if we leave it now, having done no more than pass before us the scene and its meaning.

According to Saint Luke, this scene arose like an exhalation from prayer. "As he prayed, the fashion of his countenance was altered." It was one of those occasions of designed, deliberate, lengthened, and most exalted communion with the Father. "He took Peter and John and James, and went up into a mountain to pray. And as he prayed, the fashion of his countenance was altered, and his raiment was white and glistering." This is a picture, as it were, drawn by God, of prayer and its results. And oh that we would know once for all that the outside is nothing to the inside, and that transfigurations far more divine than this sight to the eye take place wherever true prayer rises to God!

Observe also, for your consolation, ye who have buried the dead from your sight, and who yourselves must soon be numbered with them, the image here of the resurrection and of resurrection bodies. See this body the same, yet how changed! and wrought as naturally as you have seen a dark and ragged mass of vapor in the heavens pass into an object of splendor fit to be an ornament to that place where dwells the very presence of the Majesty on high. "So also is the resurrection of the dead. It is sown in corruption; it is raised in incorruption: it is sown in dishonor; it is raised in glory." Yes, fellow-mortals, some of us at least shall be transfigured like this; for "we know that when he shall appear, we shall be like him; for we shall see him as he is," — and not only like this splendid transfigured person, but with him: "Father, I will that they also whom thou hast given me be with me where I am."

I have said that the sacredness of the old Hebrew Testament was signified in the feeling of Peter as to the common glory of all the three great figures before him: "And as they departed from him, Peter said unto Jesus, Master, it is good for us to be here: and let us make three tabernacles; one for thee, and one for Moses, and one for Elias." But I reserved to the last the way in which this scene was so contrived as to give the most sublime eminence to Christ. Listen: "While Peter thus spake," — while he was eagerly soliciting tabernacles for all, — "there came a cloud, and a voice out of the cloud, saying, This is my beloved Son: hear him," — that is, not Elias and Moses and Christ. This is the King; this is He — this; no servant, no mere delegate, however imperial; this is a Son; "my Son;" "my beloved Son: hear him." Silence, all other voices; silence, the voices of lawgivers and sages through all antiquity; silence, ye illustrious leaders of the people of God; silence, Sinai. There is another voice, which "shall not strive, nor cry, neither shall any man hear his voice in the streets." Listen: "The Spirit of the Lord is upon me, because he hath anointed me to preach the gospel to the poor; he hath sent me to heal the broken-hearted, to preach deliverance to the captives, and recovering of sight to the blind, to set at liberty them that are bruised, to preach the acceptable year of the Lord."

We are sinful men; we are grown hard in secularity, in sorrows, in sins; but at that still, small voice of hope and tenderness we stop. Yes, Master; speak on, thou voice of mercy! Speak down into the depths of all human sorrow and sin and hopelessness and fears. Speak with that voice which raises even the dead.

Friends, many questions may be asked about you, but there is only one of import. Are you listeners to the voice of the Son of God? All duties may be gathered up into one. Do we obey the voice which spake out of the cloud on the Mount of Transfiguration? Listen to the resting and strengthening words. Down in the depths of human sin, of human trial, of human sorrow and hopelessness, — in all that cloud of evil and of fear in which mortality is sunk, that voice of the Father always breaks out of the cloud: "This is my beloved Son; hear him."

V.

THE LORD'S SUPPER.

This is my body. — LUKE xxii. 19.

IF we did not see every day that men give to the language and acts of one another a color varying almost indefinitely, according to the tone and views of their own minds, — if we were not accustomed to this, we should be astonished at the wide difference of opinion in the Christian world as to the meaning of the New Testament.

It is not the difference of religious opinions which has made such sad havoc in the Church, but the spirit with which these differences are maintained. So long as there are peculiarities among men, there will be certain degrees and aspects of doctrine better fitted to one class than another. The truly desirable unity in the Christian Church consists not in this, that all men should interpret sacred Scripture in precisely the same way. No; the unity to be longed for is a unity of spirit, and that Christian people should improve themselves in candor, forbearance, humility, and love, and thus educe a higher unity out of all differences.

These remarks are naturally suggested by the text, "This is my body." As to what the Saviour meant when he instituted his supper, millions of men, for several centuries, have disputed, and the fiercest controversy is to this day waged concerning it.

One of the chief distinctions of the Roman Catholic Church is their doctrine upon this subject. It is very precisely expressed in one word, Transubstantiation, — a word first applied to it by Stephen, Bishop of Autun, — that it is the real body and blood. Their evidence for this they find in the words of Christ. He does indeed call the bread his body, — "This is my body;" just in the same style, however, as "This is the Lord's passover," "Which rock was Christ."

Our Lord uses the very same figure when speaking of truth in general, or of his truth: "I am the bread of life: he that cometh to me shall never hunger, and he that believeth on me shall never thirst." In the same style he tells the woman of Samaria that whosoever would drink of the water that he should give him should thirst no more. He seems to have provided against any such interpretation as this, by eating and drinking of the body and blood while as yet he sat by their side.

I do not say that the doctrine is contradictory to our faculties; I have never thought so, though the large mass of Catholics and most Protestants view it in such a way as would certainly make it so. According to the ordinary view of Transubstantiation, the bread and wine are changed at once into all properties of the body and blood of Christ, and yet are in some respect bread and wine. This would be to disbelieve the eyes and taste, and to deny reason. But many Roman Catholic theologians state the doctrine in less exceptionable terms; namely, that the transubstantiation does not occur in the ordinary properties of the bread and wine, but in that substance, or something, which underlies all the properties of matter,— that it is which is changed from the substance of bread into the substance of Christ's body.

Although this may be an entirely incorrect philosophy, which separates between the substance of matter and its properties, yet this view of the subject removes its more obvious objections. But at the same time it really changes, if looked into, the whole doctrine, and makes that which is called matter really spirit, which can only be spiritually received. Wherever throughout the world the officiating priest utters the last syllable of the form of consecration (it is not deemed to take place until that sound), this awful change occurs. "This is my body," "This is my blood,"— at the sound of these creating or at least producing words the mighty production follows.

The strange views and evils into which this doctrine leads I will not notice. One only let me mention,— as the bread and wine become the veritable body and blood of Christ, they are from that moment, until the bread becomes corrupt and the wine dead, regarded and treated with all the adoration due to Christ himself, and so worshipped everywhere; every crumb and particle is instinct with the Godhead; raised on high on the altar with great pomp to be worshipped; carried in solemn procession to be worshipped. In the vast cathedral thousands prostrate themselves before it, and the knee is bent to it in the crowded street. Now, were it certain, according to their own views, that the real presence of Christ was in these elements, the adoration would be less painful.

But it was my purpose merely to state the different views. At the awaking of mind at the Reformation, Luther, dissatisfied with the idolatry of the bread and wine, and yet believing it to be literally true that the body and blood of Christ were present in the sacrament, devised a plan which he thought would avoid difficulties. He taught, therefore, that the body and blood were actually in the consecrated bread and wine, but in, with, and under it, and that the bread and wine remained unchanged. This is called Consubstantiation. He thus avoided the worship of the bread and wine; but in point of reason the doctrine appears to me much less defensible than that of Transubstantiation.

Zwingle, the illustrious Swiss reformer, a man second, in my opinion, to none of the reformers, and to whose name history has not done justice, — Zwingle saw clearly the weakness of Luther's view, but passing to the contrary extreme, reduced the sacrament too near to the nature of a commemorative supper. His view is approached by a very large number of Protestants, and by the Unitarians is reduced yet more; for with them, as I believe, it is strictly and only a solemn and impressive memorial of the death of Christ.

None of these views can be called entirely erroneous. Each of them ought rather to be considered either as defective only or as the exaggeration of what is really true and important. On the one hand, it is most true, as the Roman Catholic and Lutheran think, that there is a real and actual presence of Christ in this his supper. On the other hand, it is not less true, as some Protestants think, that this is a grand memorial act, — that one of its greatest purposes is to call to mind; but this is not all. Something important has been dropped.

Though we must regard both these views on either extreme as erroneous, yet they are not without this value, at least, that each gives especial and emphatic effect to some *one* aspect of the truth. But what is our view of this matter? It is a view not without great difficulties, and I do not wish to represent it otherwise. We find in our Twenty-eighth Article these two assertions: "To such as rightly, worthily, and by faith receive the same, the bread which we break is a partaking of the body of Christ, and likewise the cup of blessing is a partaking of the blood of Christ." This alone might mean Transubstantiation. Another assertion, however, is added: "The body of Christ is given, taken, and eaten in the supper only after a heavenly and spiritual manner; and the mean whereby the body of Christ is received and eaten in the supper is *Faith*."

Now, although there is some appearance of confusion in this language, it certainly means two things, — that while the *whole* is a spiritual proceeding, yet it still in some way puts us in possession of and union with the body and blood of Christ; that we eat but the consecrated bread and wine, and yet in doing that are united to the whole person of Christ, body as well as soul. This will not appear contradictory if it be thus explained: by the sensible effect of bread and wine presenting vividly to the imagination the Saviour broken and bleeding, — by this, and by the special promise of God, believers in the sacrament are spiritually united to Christ in an emphatic and eminent degree: their spirit to his. A transubstantiation takes place, but a far more profound one than a change of body, — a changing over of the very substance of the believer's spirit into that of his Lord. This union, thus begun in the spirit, has in it the germ of a union extending down through the whole nature, even by the force of the one divine Spirit, which is able to subdue all things even unto itself. In the words of Archbishop Secker: "The pious and virtuous receiver eats the flesh and drinks the blood, in the sense that he shared in the life and strength derived from his incarnation and death, and through faith in him becomes by a vital union one with him." Or we might go further: it is through this spirit only, which will work out all its results in due season, — it is through it that we become "members," as the apostle says, "of his body, of his flesh, and of his bones."

Though no one may conceive rightly as to the mode, it seems clear enough that no other view fully satisfies Scripture language, which on the one hand requires (if we give it anything like its due and natural force) the most intimate union conceivable between Christ and his people, and on the other hand requires no less that the union be not a gross communication of body and blood, but spiritual, or at least begun in spirit.

When, therefore, the emblem of the broken body is placed in the hand of the humble and penitent believer, and he hears the voice of his divine Master saying to him, "This is my body, broken for you," let him realize vividly the presence and forgiveness and love of his Saviour, and surrender his whole being, body, soul, and spirit, into communion and union with him.

I have now stated as well as I could in so small a space the different opinions of this ordinance, and what we suppose is the true view of it. Let me briefly advert to some of the benefits of it. But these are in no wise to be attained by those who lightly or unadvisedly come to this holy feast. There must be consideration, self-examination, unfeigned sorrow for sin, and a humble faith in the Lord Jesus, "whose blood cleanseth from all sin." Without this temper, we but eat and drink judgment to ourselves. I do not say "damnation" to ourselves, as it is in our version, for that by common consent is not the proper translation of the word, and is so awful as only to be fitted to discourage or even destroy the soul.

Approaching, then, in a fit temper of mind this holy communion, we shall surely find, as I have said, its benefits to be great. Nothing could be devised which is a greater assistance to the weakness of faith. We as it were "touch and taste and handle" the Word of life; the great Sacrifice once offered for the sins of the world is placed in our midst. Here, too, is a lesson of humility and penitence most impressive. Here is the Son of God set forth as made a sin-offering for us. The scene of the crucifixion is lived over again, and we look upon him whom we have pierced, and wail because of him! It is to this mind that God would bring us. Prayer made to him will then be answered.

> "A broken heart, my God, my King,
> Is all the sacrifice I bring;
> The God of grace will ne'er despise
> A broken heart for sacrifice."

But it is not only or chiefly a feast of sorrow; it is a feast of joy, a sacrament of thanksgiving and hope and love. As to thankfulness and hope, in our church service we find that this is ranked as the first and highest of all the acts of worship which the occasion should call forth.

With joy should we take the cup of salvation. We are admitted to drink of the wells of eternal life. We are admitted to mystical union with Christ. What unspeakable gifts are freely, sensibly offered to all, even to the vilest of sinners. The hopeless, the outcast returning homeward, see here hung out the signals and pledges of peace, of forgiving love, of reconciliation and restoration.

Besides these things, this is the great sacrament of love. "Herein was love, that this man laid down his life for his friends." To perpetuate forever before the eyes of the race the sight of his dead body, broken for us, and thus to melt into deepest tenderness the heart, — this was the great purpose of the institution. "This do in remembrance of me." There is in this more to draw and chain the human heart to duty than all the systems of morality ever devised. "If a man love me, he will keep my words."

VI.

THE CRUCIFIXION.

It was the third hour, and they crucified him. — MARK xv. 25.

THE law of suffering and effort as a condition of the evolution of character, and of its exhibition and influence, I take to be the widest and deepest law under which all spirits stand. God has prepared a great spectacle of suffering. Why? No suffering is fortuitous, — that God doth not willingly afflict is a great truth, — least of all the suffering of Christ. Why, then?

First, his sufferings were necessary, not only to manifest but also to originate that excellence which seems most divine to our conceptions, and which is, in fact, a new type of the nature of the invisible God. I mean that God, viewed as giving his Son to suffer, and the Son of God viewed as suffering, present an image of moral or divine excellence unspeakably above any other image of the divine nature it is possible for us to think of, and that suffering was the necessary condition through which this exhibition originated and was made. I view the agony of Calvary as the means of a new era in the manifestation of God, in that it presented the divine nature in the position (in some real sense) of trial, of exigency, of painful and indescribable effort in behalf of the creature. "He learned obedience by the things which he suffered." He was made "perfect through sufferings."

Secondly, the sufferings of Christ were intended to be of infinite value to man as a solace for his miseries in the loneliness of the human soul, especially in its deeper experiences, — and as a guide, incentive, and benign exemplar through the difficulties of his life and death. "We have not an high priest which cannot be touched with the feeling of our infirmities."

Thirdly, these sufferings of Jesus Christ were the penalty for the sins of mankind. He was set forth as a sacrifice, the Lamb slain in our place and for us. I do not mean that Christ bore in himself the penalty that we should have borne. Abhorred be the thought that he should feel in his soul any consciousness of guilt, any agony of remorse! Divinely innocent Sufferer, far be that from thee! The weak and false fancies of men have made this divine Lamb to bear our precise penalty, both as to the sort of suffering and the degree of it. As to the nature of these sufferings, and how they availed to our acquittance, we can say nothing at present. It is sufficient to know that they were borne purely for us, and that the result of them is freedom, life, salvation, unconditioned and unstinted, to every one who believes.

In view of all this, I say that the right feeling and comprehension of the sufferings of Jesus Christ constitute the whole of the Gospel of God. It is the special will of God that we should deliberately contemplate it. This is our warrant for intruding into precincts so sacred.

If I were not forbidden by Christianity to do so, I should suppose the fact of the necessity of suffering reached up even to the divine nature itself, — that God's purposes, in common with those of all the creatures made in his image, could only be worked out by sacrifice, by losing the life and finding it again, by effort, through a dark element which is against. Look around you: God certainly seems to be painfully laboring under a heavy opposition in matter and in soul. "The whole creation," and the Creator with it, seems to be "groaning and travailing in pain together until now." Indeed, the sacred Scriptures do not entirely deny such a hostile element, opposing, and as if frustrating, the divine work itself, for the very name Satan signifies *that which is against,* — *the opposer ;* and the New Testament represents that the mastery over that mysterious adverse power is to be effected only ultimately, and through infinite sacrifice.

This is in accordance with some of the latest results of our modern thought, the conclusions of human philosophy seeming to place us substantially on the same grounds with early revelation. All deliverance, I repeat, is through suffering and blood. We at least are all born to suffer, and to reach, if we reach at all, through trial; and this whether for ourselves or for others. It is the divine material out of which a new creation may be made, clear as silver or diamond; for all our evils may be turned into self-sacrifice, and all self-sacrifice is victory and glory and honor.

Now in this we — nay, the whole mass of struggling souls — are a wide image of him, the Captain of all salvation, who rendered himself up to death, purified himself through the things which he suffered, and purified and saved others through the same self-sacrifice and love. Take these last scenes: see how the Redeemer emerges through them. The evangelists, as if sensible that the revelation and power of the Son of God were greatest at the end, and in proportion to exigencies and trial, here expand these in order that divine self-sacrifice may be seen, and may redeem the spirit of the world.

What these sufferings were not can be better told than what they were. To be poor, to be unknown, to suffer much physical discomfort, to be humiliated, as we say, were in themselves no great trials to the Son of God. If he was "from above, and above all," this sort of trial would bring no heavy sacrifice to him. He had at times no place to lay his head; but he liked to feel that though "the foxes have holes, and the birds of the air have nests, the Son of man" had no place "to lay his head" but upon the bosom of the Father. Others were fretted by hunger, others would have admired Martha for attending to their comforts; but he thought Mary had chosen the better part. His meat was to do the will of him that sent him, and to finish his work.

Many will think that his obscurity on the earth, the neglect of the high, were burning humiliations for the Son of God; but what to his majesty were the opinions and honors of a mass of such beings as we are? His chief sorrows were not of this sort. The sufferings of his crucifixion were partly, no doubt, from the keen pangs of a body peculiarly sensitive to physical pain, but chiefly even then, I think, from the perfection of his heart. If we would have a comprehensive idea of the things which he suffered, we must think of what he was. If we think, for example, of his relations to the Father, and think of cloud and doubt hiding the Father's face; if we think of his relations to man, — he their Saviour, and yet there the surging sea of deviltry, swaying and dashing and hissing at his feet, these things will give us some idea of the depth of his sufferings. Beyond this I enter not into the consideration of them; yet I feel the beauty and force of that petition in the Greek liturgy, "By thy *unknown* sorrows, good Lord, deliver us."

We now approach the last scene. I will omit the stupendous denial of Peter in the high priest's hall, when he said with cursing and oaths that he did not know the man. I will not dwell upon the fact that they all forsook him and fled, or upon the scenes called the trials of Christ, of which there were certainly four and perhaps six, — scenes of unparalleled outrage, in which the victim was awfully harassed and racked. I must omit his divine demeanor through all this, saying, however, that God so arranged that when the Son appeared the Jew appeared at his side, to test and bring out by an ideal cruelty the ideal glory of the soul of Christ. There they stood together and will stand, they discovering him and he discovering them.

It seems to me that God intended to set forth this greatest of transactions by the most wonderful methods that could be devised. He places before us that head on which there are many crowns, covered with a crown of thorns; he shows us a reed in the hand which forever holds the sceptre of the world, — him whose train fills the temple of all this earth coming forth in a mock purple robe, and the eye blindfolded which saw God.

But look especially at his patience and silence. The apostle James seems particularly struck with his patience, his fathomless endurance: "Ye have heard of the patience of Job, and have seen the end of the Lord." "He did oppose his patience to their fury, and armed himself to suffer, with a quietness of spirit, the very rage and tyranny of theirs." Hope, though usually and singularly paramount in him, is absent through these last scenes. It was simple endurance. I remember but one distinct forward look of hope: "I will not drink henceforth of this fruit of the vine, until that day when I drink it new with you in my Father's kingdom."

Then his silence. His judges, Pilate above all, felt

this silence with awe. That a man should make no effort for his life filled them with astonishment and fear. But he, knowing that words would avail nothing, was silent, and left it to his cross, to his blood, to his grave, to speak.

When Pilate found he could not save him but by some sacrifice to himself, he gave the fatal order for the crucifixion, the fatal command, "Ibis ad crucem." He is condemned; and in a few moments all is made ready for departure to the place of death.

Of the way to the cross we know little. The Church of the Middle Ages has well called it the Via Dolorosa, and filled the way with tragic traditions all unknown to us. But this we know, — that Jesus could not bear his cross, as criminals were required to do; probably fell under it, and probably was urged and scourged forward, but certainly could carry it no longer. We must remember that he was weakened by suffering and the terrible scourging to which he had been subjected. I must notice here that the Gospels, so far from exaggerating, give the barest outlines of the chief facts. They say next to nothing about the passage to Calvary. Saint Luke, however, does tell us what we are glad to hear, — that amid all this carnival of hell, in the surging of that crowd of enemies or silent friends, there were "women, which also bewailed and lamented him."

Arrived at last, the cross-beams are nailed together, and while they are lying on the ground the victim is nailed to them. Then, "Father, forgive them; they know not what they do." The cross is raised, and with a shock dropped into its hole and firmly planted. There he hung, dying, from nine o'clock until three. The crisis was "about the ninth hour," when he cried with a loud voice, saying, "Eli! Eli! lama sabacthani? that is to say, My God! My God! why hast thou forsaken me?" Man first forsook him,—"they all forsook him and fled,"—but now, at last, he is forsaken of God. *Why* hast thou forsaken me? *Thou* for whose love I am here, art thou gone too?

Judge his trial when that faith, that trust, which he had without measure, seemed to crumble in his bosom. He was left alone, as if without God or hope, and so descended into the dark, crying again with an exceeding loud voice. If that were so, even while it opens a gulf of horror which we dare not look down into, do not think that in him the faith of faithfulness was gone, though the glad and enjoying trust of the Son of man was gone for that moment. God was still "My God;" he was a God looked to, appealed to, adjured; and though it was a trial which had gone so deep that it tore away the soul, its glad faith, its peace, its hope, still it left the heart in the midst of the infinite ruin, true, clinging to God to the last gasp.

But what a scene! There are two great centres of darkness in the history of these sufferings: first, "My soul is exceeding sorrowful, even unto death;" second, *this*, and this above all,—that cup which was pressed to his lips in Gethsemane, and which was so bitter that he said, " If it be possible, let this cup pass from me," is pressed to his lips again. Drink, Son of man, drink to the dregs; it is death to you, but it is salvation to all.

The evangelists say that Nature suffered a revolution, that the earth was dark, and the great "veil of the temple was rent in twain from the top to the bottom [as if to open the path from sinful man to his God], and the earth did quake, and the rocks rent, and the graves were opened." And it surely ought to have been so. The spiritual world seemed broken up; why not the natural? The Lamb of God is dead, trod out of the earth and forsaken of God. So it seemed. The light must darken in the heavens, Nature must cry out, and the earth must wail because of him, as one waileth for an only son.

And now I ask, *Why* all this? Sin! sin! God was behind, allowing the law of sorrow to do its work of deliverance and redemption in the bosom of the Son of God, — that law which prepares life through death; that law which purified the highest through the things which he suffered, and through him redeemed all the souls which really behold him. And, oh joy! though sunk so low, the height in purity and power to which he rose was exactly correspondent to the depth to which he went down; and when he finished his great cry, " Eli! " the everlasting crown was placed upon his head, and the redemption of the earth was begun, established. Shall not the death of the Lord break the power of sin in us and in all?

"Surely he hath borne our griefs, and carried our sorrows: he was wounded for our trangressions, he was bruised for our iniquities: the chastisement of our peace was upon him; and with his stripes we are healed. All we like sheep have gone astray; we have turned every one to his own way; and the Lord hath laid on him the iniquity of us all."

VII.

EASTER.

He is risen; he is not here: behold the place where they laid him. — MARK xvi. 1.

HERE is the announcement of an angel to simple women. It is singular (I do not speak it in praise, but merely as a fact), — the prominence of women in the Gospels, and their natural affinity to Christ and Christianity in all ages. No; not singular, but instructive and impressive. A woman washed his feet with tears. A woman said of him, "Come, see a man which told me all things that ever I did: is not this the Christ?" Women followed him and ministered to him. Two women were among his closest friends. During the last scene women wept him and also bewailed him. It is pleasing to think that when all else deserted him and fled, the tears of women gave some natural solace to his heart. And we read that at the moment when all was just over, there were women "looking on afar off;" and there were others, as Saint John states it, just under the cross, — as near, I presume, as the soldiers would let them be; and in this company (whether standing near or standing off) were Mary Magdalene and Mary the mother of James, "and many other women which came up with him unto Jerusalem." It was quite a noticeable fact. And these women kept near, it seems, after life had left him, and watched the descent from the cross, and watched all that was done; and when at last Joseph took the body to his tomb, two of them followed and watched. And at last "Mary Magdalene and Mary the mother of Joses beheld where he was laid." And then, I presume, they departed. But when the Sabbath was past, these women, having bought some sweet and costly spices (though they were but poor), came that they might anoint him, and to *them* the first word of the new life came.

Through the week just past we have followed Jesus up to his cross and his sepulchre, and have seen him dead who was the life of the world. All things seem to have declared for wrong and for supreme cruelty; and holiness and love hung nailed to the cross. It has been "the hour and power of darkness." The crowd dispersed, the priests, much pleased, went back to the temple. The governor was in his palace. On yesterday, which was the Jewish sabbath, the priests and elders and people thronged the courts of the temple; the blood of two hundred thousand lambs — the usual number — was shed, incense rose, and the grand and solemn worship of the Jews was celebrated. Jesus is dead; the real Paschal Lamb is sacrificed; and a dusky figure — some Satanic Power — has sat down on the throne! But — but "very early in the morning, the first day of the week," certain women "came unto the sepulchre at the rising of the sun;" and some one said unto them: "Be not affrighted: ye seek Jesus of Nazareth, which was crucified: he is risen; he is not here: behold the place where they laid him." If the earth quaked at his death, the heavens themselves should have broken open at that announcement!

This, then, is the morning of the resurrection. The first day of the era of new life for us and for all creatures has begun. Of this fact I might offer positive and elaborate evidence, attesting directly and indirectly and multitudinously; but it is not necessary. I might show also the harmony of the event with all facts, with all truths, with all human wants. I might show you its justice, its mercy, its beauty, — that it is the desire and the demand of the groaning world. I might show its power. Nay, far more than that. Look at the contrary: if Christ is *not* risen, — if he is gone, sunk; if his last wail is *forever* true, that God has forsaken him, — then, I say, that fact has added a weight *against* God, against the character, against the very being of God, — has added somewhat against him which is as deep as the earth and wide as the sea! But the news is that Christ is risen! He is not holden of death! The enigmas of Providence and the world — the central darkness — is lit up as by lightnings. The news is that injustice and wickedness are shown to be but for a moment, and that the right shall have dominion in the morning! The news is that to those who have the spirit of Christ there are properly no more such things as evil and death. Blessed are they, for they shall have part in his resurrection, and upon them no death shall have power.

If this is true, was there ever heard such news? For if Christ live forevermore, it is possible, probable, pledged indeed, that we shall live forevermore. He is but "the first-fruits of them that slept." Just as the Jews plucked the first delicate corn and grass and fruits and carried them up to the Lord, so he was carried up in this springtime of Easter, as a sign and pledge of the great harvest of the dead coming after.

If Christ be not risen, every dead body preaches annihilation; or, at least, a deep shadow rests upon the grave. Spite of all the little proofs, little hopes of men, "it still remains true that there is but little hope, — that the last known and recorded thing of the strongest man is his weakness, of the wisest man is the failure of his powers, of the best man that he has suffered the punishment of sin." Science would leave the world as it was left when Christ said, "Eli! Eli! lama sabacthani?" But now we see Christ risen, and the great things of hope have become the great things of fact, of experience. "God hath both raised up the Lord, and will also raise us up by his own power."

It is very easy to talk of the resurrection — of the boundless relief of the resurrection — in some half-flippant way. Do I feel it? Do I know — have I ever reflected — what the state of man is without Christ raised; without the hopes of this morning? All our souls, their highest and their natural instincts, yearn for and demand continuance. The whole race demands a rising again. But without Christ risen there is not only no certainty of immortality for us, but many presumptions against it. Christ perished, unraised, unvindicated, with the wail of desertion on his lips, — that does not leave things as he found them; that darkens the old hope, darkens God, and leaves us to the doctrine of death. We will die as the beasts; and why not? We are creatures like the insects, — here we are to-day, to-morrow passed as a mist, — without Christ. I know not how long man has been upon the earth, but long enough for us to know that the generations are but shadows. Oh, our nothingness! Take the town we live in. Though it is only of yesterday, yet it seems very old and sad when we think of the people who have passed through it, — these very streets occupied and emptied so many times. We are dream-people.

Yearning for life, but sinking in death, what hope is there? As the world goes on, the hope for us does not increase! The race advances, but the hope for each man does not advance. After all that modern thought and discovery have reached, the light around the grave thickens. Among our discoveries we cannot discover immortality. "The vulture's eye hath not seen it." So, in this dark and gloom of Nature, we cry like children in the night; we cry aloud, "Is there any hope?" What answer? Listen! Nothing but silence. That silence is our answer. Like a ship on fire and sinking at sea, we glance for aid from horizon to horizon; but over and through this frightful waste no help, no man, no God appears, and we are about dumbly to sink, each in his turn, like lead into the waters. There is no hope; it is all guess. Such is the state of facts without the Easter morning. I repeat, then, that there never was such news as the news of to-day! The Captain, the Precursor, has gone through! He has shown us the path of life; and the redeemed race, dying with him, will forever live with him.

I wish I knew how to speak about such a fact. Only a few of us are real and deep believers. If we did believe we would rejoice, and our miserable lives would be raised up at once. If we did believe, our feeble, failing virtue, always needing fresh strength, would find it here. Our cares and sorrows, always needing fresh consolations, would find them here. Why is it that, standing in such awful need of this fact, we do not grasp it, and give to ourselves some joy on earth? Why? The secret reason is that we know that, to rise as Christ did, we must, like him, "first die to sin and live to righteousness." It was the heavenly and powerful spirit of Christ — "the life to righteousness " — which raised him up; it was by and through the Eternal Spirit that was in him, which was too strong for death, as the apostle says; and it is by sharing in the same spirit that we also shall rise. This we do not seem to know. Nor do we know the reverse, — that the man who does not share in the spirit of Christ cannot share the resurrection of life, for one follows the other. The resurrection morning, then, can only be a joy to those who have at least the beginnings of Christ's spirit in them, — " Christ formed in them the hope of glory." There must be first a resurrection of real life in the human heart before, and in order to, the resurrection of the body.

But we don't think enough of this resurrection of our hearts; we don't think much of the passing from evil to good, from death to life, in the spirit and at this moment; we don't think enough of the triumph of a good thought and feeling over an evil, — to repress hatred by forgiveness, — and that our hearts, like the dissolving lights, should pass from pictures of earth to those of heaven, and all that is small give place to that which is noble; but we think the resurrection of the *body* a great matter. We say, " Oh yes; the great resurrection ! "

We mistake. The greatness is in the change of the spirit. It is possible, I think probable, perhaps necessary, that the pure spirit of a man, when once formed over into the likeness of Christ, will, in its long history to come (for we believe that it grows), take to itself a thousand successive or numberless bodies, — always, in a sense, the same body, as the spirit is always the same spirit, — but each body in its details passing away, as the spirit becomes ready for a higher form and needs it. So that the spirit in us, once raised, — that is, come out from the death of sin now and here, — this is that *first resurrection*, compared with which all bodily resurrections are secondary, and will follow as a matter of course whenever the gradual enlargement of the soul needs them.

I say, then, that every good affection felt in the heart, every good will, every confiding feeling towards the Redeemer of our spirits, is the beginning in us of the noblest resurrection. We must, then, begin to live in our hearts, and then as certainly as Christ lives we shall live also: death is utterly abolished.

Don't think lightly of the heart. Learn to estimate the value of it by this, — that it is the beginning and fountain of all resurrections. Deny, then, and reject the wrongs of your heart, for that is the resurrection of death, and turn to those opposite feelings which in fact are the resurrection feelings of life, which are so deep in vitality and value that they must bloom out into eternal life.

The truth I teach is: Your body must go with your spirit; if the one is alive, the other will be alive also. To you, then, who wish to trust in the divine mercy, and would begin at this moment to be what your heart tells you you ought to be, — rejoice! Your resurrection begins now, and the resurrection of the body awaits you. This is the day the Lord hath made. The cry of joy is in the tabernacles of the righteous. Christ is risen.

VIII.

THE ASCENSION.

And it came to pass, while he blessed them, he was parted from them, and carried up into heaven. — LUKE xxiv. 51.

WE have commemorated the resurrection of Christ. We now commemorate the ascension of Christ. It is well perhaps, as a matter of custom, to review annually these great and interesting facts; and what is wanting in freshness in such subjects should be supplied by the permanent importance they must ever possess to all mankind.

This event did not take place until forty days after the resurrection and ten days before the Pentecost. It seems at first a very strange fact that the risen Lord should remain for that period of time among men, — among them and yet not of them. Some have supposed that his body was passing in that time through "a slow and physical purification to be meet for ascending;" but such reasons are rather curious than probable. Still, there were *good* reasons for it. It was of the utmost importance, for instance, thoroughly to convince and instruct the minds of those who were to be the founders of the Church. His appearance among them might have seemed a delusion if it had occurred

THE ASCENSION.

only in one day or a few days. It might then have come to be ranked with many wonderful stories — as to the seeing of spirits. But to see him through so long a time as forty days must have given his followers a sort of certainty and familiarity with the fact which nothing could shake. This is intimated by Saint Luke: "He showed himself alive after his passion by many infallible proofs, being seen of them forty days." Nothing could have so assuring an effect as time. Besides, he spent this time in opening their understandings and speaking to them of the things pertaining to the kingdom of God. He taught them the ancient prophecies as to himself, beginning at Moses and all the prophets; he showed them the meaning of his mission on earth, — that Christ *ought* to have suffered these things, and then to enter into his glory. More than this: he imbued them with the spirit of his religion. One of the reasons that they so slowly believed his resurrection (for he had clearly told them he would rise) was that they could not believe the Messiah could have such a poor, quiet, unimposing resurrection. Their idea of the resurrection was that it was to be a magnificent jubilee, at which the Messiah should call up the venerated forefathers of their race, and the splendors of his kingdom begin. Such a notion was not easily uprooted.

Again: he informed them during this time of the future and their own conduct in it. I think we have very little impression in general of the amount of our Lord's teachings when on earth, and especially little,

I think, do we know of all that he said and did during these forty days. "There are also," says John, "many other things which Jesus did, the which, if they should be written every one, I suppose that even the world itself could not contain the books that should be written."

Thus, having proved all things and ordered all things, he was ready to ascend. He had corrected and enlightened their understandings; he had roused their affections; he had solaced their hearts, infusing courage and hope; he had prepared for the important future; and so he was ready, and then only ready, to ascend.

He, being with the disciples in some private place in Jerusalem, first laid a strict and peculiar charge upon them, — that they should not depart from that city until there they received the full effusion of the Holy Spirit. Having done this, he led out the company to Mount Olivet, a short distance from Jerusalem. It was at the base of this mountain that the garden of Gethsemane lay, in which he had lately endured his sufferings; there he had been apprehended as a malefactor, and there, or on the elevated ground just above, he was now to be exalted to heaven as a Prince and King.

On the top of that mount, below and near which lay the city and temple, surrounded by a company, perhaps a few and perhaps as many as five hundred, he gave his parting commands, and lifting up over them those hands which were never raised save in benediction, he for the last time solemnly blessed them. "And it came to pass, while he blessed them, he was parted from them, and carried up into heaven."

As "he blessed them, he was parted from them." If this were a mere poetic conception, nothing could be conceived more beautifully. In what fine harmony is it with all his life! "On earth peace, good-will to men," was the first utterance spoken of him; from his childhood the very atmosphere about him seemed a perpetual and tender benediction; and his last gesture, the last sound from his sacred lips, was still blessing.

As one of the objects of this his public ascent was to convince, it was no doubt done in the clearest manner. It seems probable that he was slowly and in a stately manner wafted from them while the last words of his blessing were falling from his lips. So, gradually, he rose until a cloud above "received him out of their sight. And while they looked steadfastly toward heaven as he went up, behold, two men stood by them in white apparel, which also said, Ye men of Galilee, why stand ye gazing up into heaven? this same Jesus which is taken up from you into heaven, shall so come in like manner as ye have seen him go into heaven."

Their attention turned in this touching manner from the sorrow of parting to the joy of an expected meeting and permanent reunion with the beloved Master, the company gradually left the spot, their hearts impressed at once with the deepest sorrow and the most exulting hopes.

THE ASCENSION.

Thus was finished the earthly career of Jesus Christ the Son of God, "whom the heaven must receive until the times of restitution of all things." "Lift up your heads, O ye gates; and be ye lift up, ye everlasting doors; and the King of glory shall come in."

And now let me briefly remind you of some of those lessons which this event teaches. In the first instance, if, as I endeavored to prove to you, the resurrection of Christ gives solid evidence of two great facts, namely, the immortality of man, and the final triumph of holiness and right, then the ascension is in the highest degree the completion of that evidence; for in this we see that the power of death was not only overcome, but overcome permanently; and that goodness was rewarded in the person of Christ, not only by his freedom from death, but also by his exaltation to glory.

We must view Christ as the representative in a sense of the whole race, and the perfect image of those who follow his steps. Every good man in the sufferings of life and in the penalty of death does partake with Christ, in some degree, of that curse which he bore for all; and in like manner shall those who are truly one with him, grafted in by a living faith, rise up from death, for it is impossible that they should now be holden by it. They too, I say, must in like manner and by the same spirit emerge from the grave and the gate of death; and not only that, but, still joined and made one with him in his wonderful destiny, must pass, as he passed, into the highest place, to meet inconceivable rewards and to penetrate into an inconceivable glory.

With these inducements would that, like him, we could tread firmly in the steps of duty, running "with patience the race that is set before us, looking unto Jesus, who for the joy that was set before him, endured the cross, despising the shame, and is set down at the right hand of the throne of God."

Again, consider the fact that he went into that higher state with a human body. This wonderful fact, like most others in the New Testament, was foreshadowed by something of a similar nature. "Enoch was translated that he should not see death," Elijah was swept away in what seemed a chariot of fire, but in both these instances there is an air of distance and remoteness which makes them seem unreal.

It appears to me that if even the Son of God, who is eminently a spirit, is represented as existing really embodied in the heavenly state, — if it was the intention to impress this most forcibly by taking him away in that form before our eyes, — then we ought to shape our ideas of the future state so as to correspond with this. Must not that be a state, spiritualized indeed, but still one in which we are to appear in real bodies, and as inhabitants of a real external world? I wonder much that any one should be able to think the contrary. When we see him, says the apostle, we shall be like him; and one point of that likeness is to be the possession of an entire humanity in body as well as spirit.

You can realize then, if you will, from this ascent of the body of him who is our Forerunner, the same thing which shall actually take place in respect to us, when all those who sleep in the dust of the earth shall hear his voice and arise, and shall enter upon a state of vivid realities, bodily as well as spiritual.

Think now how delightful a fact this is, — that Christ has ascended in the human form. What a dignity does it lend to every part of our humanity, that in a human body Christ sits at the head of all power, — that all intelligent beings, however high, shall associate with that form, and with all who wear it, an interest, an attraction, of the most peculiar character; so that all who appear in it shall draw forth at once to themselves the love and joy of all other creatures! Think, too, what high capacities will belong to it when it shall be a temple fit for the Lord, the King, to dwell in! Think of what enjoyments it must be susceptible when it shall be the very likeness of him who for his sufferings is in that very form reaping the highest joys! What a triumph over the thought of death does this give the believer! Death to him shall destroy nothing, but shall recreate everything in a higher form. If our faith had force, we should look through the sorrow, the gloom, the destruction of death, as through a short vista opening on a scene of which this is but the image, that the reality; this as if the shadow of the sweet heavens when reflected in dim and troubled water, — that, those heavens themselves in their solid, eternal beauty and peace.

In asserting the likeness of the after-glory of the believer to that of Christ, of course I have not intended to make the degree of this glory similar. Of him it is said that ascending he went higher than the heavens, far above all of them, into the holiest, into the magnificent or most excellent glory, and there sat down at the right hand of Majesty, from thence expecting or waiting until all enemies shall be put under his feet.

Let us reflect for a moment on this his peculiar glory. Sitting down at the right hand of God is of course a figure by which we are to understand taking the place of power and dignity, and particularly the place of rule or administration as the chief officer of a kingdom, into whose hands all affairs are committed. From that ascension-day all things were put in subjection to him, — the ministry of angels, of men, and of events. "In him all fulness dwells." "The government" is fully "upon his shoulder." "There was given him dominion, and glory, and a kingdom, that all people, nations, and languages should serve him."

Christ there in the seat of power, his eye beholding, his hand controlling all events, — think of it. Nay, it is almost allowable to picture him to the eye, for there is nothing vague or inconceivable now as to him who rules: it is Christ, he who was born in Bethlehem of Judea and lived here under this sun and moon a few hundred years ago. He is the Ruler. You cannot be in danger of thinking it too real. He is there to whose wisdom as a ruler, to whose mild justice as a judge, to whose tenderness as a guardian and protector we may all commit ourselves in every event of life with the deepest assurance and peace.

It is a great thought that Jesus Christ is now actually our ruler, disposing everything that concerns us; and whatever event happens to us, whether it seem good or ill, — a deep and bitter grief, or prosperity, — let us always remember that that hand, last seen in benediction, has ordered it, to bring us home to himself.

The Guide of us men has not left us because he has gone away. Indeed it seems, I know not for what reason, that one of the great objects of his leaving the earth and ascending was that the power of the Spirit, and with it all good gifts, might more effectually be granted to us. "It is expedient," he says, with mournful tenderness accounting to his disciples for his absence, — "it is expedient for you that I go away; for if I go not away, the Comforter will not come unto you; but if I depart, I will send him unto you."

I say it was his purpose in ascending up on high to obtain gifts for men, which he will dispense the more liberally the more freely they are sought. Now, " whatsoever ye shall ask in my name, that will I do."

In the last place, in view of Christ's ascension we are bound to remember his reappearance,—"Whom the heaven must receive until the times of restitution of all things." He "shall so come in like manner as ye have seen him go into heaven." "In like manner," which I understand literally. He has descended in various forms since his departure: in the power of his spirit and in the power of his providence, in the consolation of his church and in the overthrow of its enemies; but he is yet, it would seem, to reappear in literal verity. He "shall so come in like manner as ye have seen him go into heaven." "Every eye shall see him." He ascended in the presence of only a few friends, whose testimony we believe; he will come again in grand publicity. "As the lightning cometh out of the east, and shineth even unto the west, so shall also the coming of the Son of man be."

To that point we are bound to look forward. It is to come. He shall be seen in the clouds of heaven, and all the holy angels with him. And what shall the purpose be of that grand visit? Why comes he in this power and great glory? He has one purpose before him: he will come to sit upon the throne of his glory, and to render to all the recompense of reward; to them who have done wickedly, "shame and everlasting contempt;" to them who have worked righteousness, "glory and honor and immortality."

To that reappearance, which in some sense certainly every eye shall see, let us all look, and for that day of the Lord make ready. Whatever it may be for others, to us let it be, weak, struggling, unworthy as we are, joy through eternity. "Come, ye blessed of my Father, inherit the kingdom prepared for you." "Ye are they which have continued with me in my temptations; and I appoint unto you a kingdom, even as my Father hath appointed unto me."

IX.

WHITSUNDAY.

If I depart, I will send him unto you. And when he is come, he will reprove the world of sin, and of righteousness, and of judgment: of sin, because they believe not on me; of righteousness, because I go to my Father, and ye see me no more; of judgment, because the prince of this world is judged. — JOHN xvi. 7-11.

CONSIDER this: a poor man and young, surrounded by a few fishermen and the like, about to suffer as a malefactor, speaking of the Sacred Spirit, of that which lies below and creates the life of the soul, as the god of the air would speak of sending his winds, or the sun-god of sending his mysterious light; speaking of this overshadowing essence which

> "Dove-like, sit'st brooding on the vast abyss,
> And mak'st it pregnant," —

of this, as directing it, despatching it from him, and for the sole purpose of revealing and exalting him, illuminating his face to the world, and circling it with a halo of unearthly lights. With no strain, or consciousness of anything unusual, he puts himself up as the director of the Sacred Spirit, and describes it as gathering around him with all its amplitudes of power and light, to subserve and to illustrate him.

Think of that, and tell me whether any alternative is left us but to say, as the Jews did, " This man hath a devil and is mad," or to say, " Truly this is the Son of God." Just think of it for yourselves, putting any meaning on it you choose.

"If I depart, I will send the Comforter unto you." And now, its offices. When this awful agent should come, it was to do three things: "He will reprove the world of sin, and of righteousness, and of judgment;" that is, show clearly the fact of sin, of righteousness, and of judgment.

I dare not change the order of these divine words of Jesus, but the three great works of the Spirit will be placed in a more natural gradation for our thoughts if we view the one here put second as the first: " He will reprove the world of righteousness, because I go to my Father, and ye see me no more."

While Christ himself was in the world he was the righteous light of the world. Since his face is removed from our eyes, and his words from our ears, the vision and the hearing of the heart must be opened, that we may see him who is now invisible; that the soul once impressed through the aid of the senses, now made susceptible, vitalized, by the new Enlightener, may commune face to face with spiritual things. Thus the first office of the Comforter was to "reprove the world of righteousness." Because the Holy One was to be removed from our eyes, its first office was to stand through all time as a substitute for the senses, as a higher sense through which we may behold and touch the glory of Christ and of all his truth. Nay, not only thus to continue the presence of the divine in the world, but to enlarge its front, and to give us a new and more inward possession of it, — to anoint the eyes to see where the light of suns has never penetrated.

We must observe how slowly were trained the disciples so long as Christ was with them, — how gradually were moulded even those chosen friends and apostles who were constantly about his person, — how ignorant and material and unpurified and Jewish they were to the last! But when with the signs of fire and with the rushing of the wind the Enlightener came, these very men stood up filled with the new wine of life, their spirits broadened, elate with grand ideas, emboldened, set on fire, so that common men — as if God were making the very stones to cry out — from that moment moved upon the world, as the Spirit within them had once moved upon the face of chaos, with a power which pervaded, disturbed, but divinely warmed and divinely reconstructed life.

So you see what mean the beautiful words, "When the Comforter is come, he will show the world clearly of righteousness, because I go to my Father, and ye see me no more." This we have seen to become a fact in the history of the world, account for it as we may. There are many things about this divine Pentecost for which it would be presumptuous in any man to attempt to account. What are all the reasons which delayed the coming of this Spirit until the body of Christ was removed, who can say? If our intelligence could see everything in the relations of the first great Spirit to our spirits and to men as a race, our thoughts would be as deep and wide as God's. Some things we can say, however. It was necessary for the humiliation of Christ that he should fulfil his course stripped to so great an extent of light and power. Again, in its operations, this Spirit, like all other power, observes many conditions, acting only according to their consent. The bodily presence of Christ as an actual man, though vital as a remembrance, was yet, in spite of all miracles, an obstacle to faith, a constant temptation to doubt and to material views.

There is a far greater difficulty, but it is common to natural religion, and appears everywhere in the world and in the history of men; namely, that, granting the existence of gracious influences, they should so limit themselves; that seeing, as we do, at Pentecost and at other epochs in the ordinary history of the world the spirit of man rising as the surface of a flood from the heaving of the oceanic depths, why the advance and recession of this divine good? Why this vast pledging of itself to hope, only to withdraw? Why, when commissioned to reprove the world of righteousness, to discover that aspect which illuminates and recreates spirits,—why to come in like a tidal wave and then retire, leaving us down at the ordinary rate of our poor existence?

I know, of course, that our own depraved wills shut God out; I know that there are reasons of moral discipline in this slowly wrought historical progress; I know also that there may be natural as there certainly are spiritual laws which control here; but still, "How long, O Lord!" is the natural cry of the heart which feels that it faints, that the race itself withers, without God. "Creation itself groaneth," waiting for the "manifestation of the Sons of God." Reprove, O Comforter, reprove the world of righteousness, because the Holy One has left us, and has gone to the Father, and we see him no more; because it is fit that all creatures should see him, that we above all, we erring and lost men, should know the expressed and redeeming God.

"When the Comforter is come, he will reprove the world of *sin* and of righteousness." This is the second great office of illumination, inherent, indeed, in the first; for when he reproves the world of righteousness, then be sure he will in that reprove us of sin.

"Of sin, because they believe not on me," — that is, because they do not appreciate and lovingly know him. Reproval of sin follows necessarily from the clear showing of righteousness, from the showing of what Christ is, the Righteous One, and so what was the state of our natures which could turn away with ignorance and distaste. That which exhibits on the one hand righteousness, or Christ as he is, exhibits just as plainly on the other what we are who cast him out. A man is as his affections, his tastes are. If we do not even know the One who, by all he is and does and has done, is justly nearest to our hearts, and who rises in divine and measureless excellence above our heads, then we are reproved of stupid blindness, of hardness, of meanness of conception, and of a will averse to the express image of perfection; and we are reproved of a depth of ingratitude and lowness, just in proportion to the cost and extent of the benefit he conferred and the height of the excellence he revealed. When, then, that discovering Spirit shines inward and shows us who this Christ is, it describes us who stand opposed, just as light defines darkness, — reveals, and so condemns us, through all the depth of our consciousness, as the unrighteous, sinners; and since all righteousness is centred and shown in him, the insensibility to it comprehends all sin.

The revelation, by the truths of philosophy, by our better instincts, by unknown influences coming through Nature or our sorrows, of a better good than we have loved or pursued, — this in the moment it is felt casts a light inward upon what we are, and backward upon what we have been; it is the tasting of a spirit which gives us instantly "to discern the madness that is in rage, the folly and the disease that are in envy," and the dishonor through the whole of us; and we stand as the first sinning parents stood when the voice of God in the garden awakened them, detected by the light, naked and ashamed. This natural experience is but the shadow of that felt when the Sacred Spirit, by drawing back the veil from the face of Christ, draws back also that veil which "lies upon our own faces, the faces of all flesh," and we see ourselves because we see him. Thus "he reproves of sin, because they believe not" in him, and thus this second great result of the Spirit—I mean the opening of self-knowledge and self-condemnation in the heart—comes necessarily of showing Christ to the heart.

The third and closing office in this grand operation is that "he will reprove the world of judgment,"—that in the very showing of sin he will condemn it; for as soon as we are made conscious of sin we are conscious of something not only corrupt, but essentially and necessarily a wrong and a usurpation, fit to be judged, which ought to be judged, which is inwardly judged, and from its own conscious weakness foreshadows its outer judgment. Sin once revealed to the soul, there is with it the revelation of a judgment-seat and a final total destruction.

The Spirit not merely reveals judgment in this way, but by showing the world clearly of Christ it shows him as not only the Righteous One, but the Overcoming One. It shows in this one history of goodness, as it appeared in time and on the earth, under every disadvantage, that where righteousness was perfectly lived it carried with it victory, even in the moment of defeat, and that death itself could not hold it, but that, triumphing openly, it ascended as a victor before the whole creation, and that therefore, as partaking of the same spirit with this first-born and Head, all men may place, as he did, all things and all power beneath their feet.

So human spirits are on the way to be freed; the race has begun the process of freedom, of divine disenthralling from the spirit of wickedness in the world, "the prince of the power of the air," as it is mysteriously and awfully called, that this, first overcome in the heart of Christ, is thence in all who are Christlike broken. The Spirit which shows this shows judgment on a scale as wide as the disorder, for it shows that the spirit of this world is judged. So when the Comforter is come he will reprove the world, bear inwardly upon the hearts of men the sense of righteousness in Christ, of their own sin, and of judgment, — judgment for sin in the heart and in the history of man, judgment upon the power of evil in the world, — "The prince of this world is judged."

And now, is all this not surely true? Do we not behold this reign of judgment in its noble beginnings? Do we not date from Christ the exalting of righteousness from the dust? Has he not given the foretaste and set on foot the impulse which shall place righteousness on every throne? Has he not come as a presence of order to all the confusion, unreason, and oppression of men, as if the voice were audible, —

"'Silence, ye troubled waves! and thou deep, peace!'
Said then the omnific Word"?

That word has been heard, believe me, and "the wild uproar stands ruled," or begins to be,— for all creations are slow.

So then hear once more the wonderful words: " If I depart, I will send him unto you. And when he is come, he will reprove the world of sin, and of righteousness, and of judgment: of sin, because they believe not on me; of righteousness, because I go to my Father, and ye see me no more; of judgment, because the prince of this world is judged."

X.

THE EXALTATION OF CHRIST.

Being made so much better than the angels, as he hath by inheritance obtained a more excellent name than they. — HEBREWS i. 4.

TRINITY SUNDAY. Trinity, tri-unity, from "trias," is a word first used in Antioch, and first found in Theophilus in the year 151. The doctrine of "Trinity" has played a great part in history, and in some sense justly, as it substantially expresses the whole doctrine of God; presenting the divine nature fully and appropriately in three great aspects, Creator, Redeemer, Sanctifier, — that is, God creating, rescuing, and uplifting; the three great offices of God. But it has been much abused, so that we may agree with Calvin when he says that he "would be willing the name of 'Trinity' should be forgotten and buried if only this much would be acknowledged by all, — that Father, Son, and Holy Spirit, each discriminated by a peculiar property, are one God." By "each being discriminated" he must mean that each is distinguished by a peculiar and deep something, which in a rough, popular way we call "personality," — that is, three persons.

I shall speak not of "Trinity," but of the New Testament views of the divinity of Christ. As far as I understand the New Testament, it sets forth Christ on the one hand as of high descent, on the other hand of high ascent, — that is, as we would express it, that he was of the divine by lineage, by blood, by birth, and that he was of the divine also by his own reach and acquirement; that he was divine by his descent, the only-begotten of God, and divine by his ascent, "perfect through suffering;" being made, having become, "better than the angels;" nay, having become so much better than they are "as he hath by inheritance obtained a more excellent name than they," — that is, his elevation over the highest spirits is obtained just as much by his own life as by his nature or descent. This seems to be the meaning of the text, the same meaning expressed by Saint Paul in his "Epistle to the Philippians," where he says, "Who, being in the form of God, thought it not robbery to be equal with God." "Wherefore," as a recompense, "God also hath highly exalted him."

This fact is noticed and dwelt upon very little, so that the Christian Church, throughout its career, has too much insisted on the glory of his inheritance, — that is, his natural elevation, — to the slighting and omitting of what he obtained, or the character and life he worked out on earth. In concerning itself so much with the natural God, with his lofty and beautiful titles as such, it forgets, or rather has not liked to remember, that peculiar and most sacred title, that he made himself " better than the angels," that his highest title was the life that he lived. It is as if some crown-prince to-day, not content with inheriting the throne, first desired to win the throne by a life corresponding to the greatness of the place to be won. The Hindoo Brahmins had the same high conception. They said, "Through earnestness did India rise to the leadership of the gods." This is a beautiful view; yet I repeat that the Church has not much dwelt upon it.

I am not much astonished, for men naturally prefer the divine by nature to the divine by achievement. Natural power, a throne in the heavens by nature and not by acquisition, that seems really Godlike; but a divine heart and will,— that seems too human, too much like us, to be altogether revered; so the Church, when thinking of the divinity of Christ, dwells more upon the natural Godship than upon the Godship of effort, the Godship of the divine man.

I know how full the Bible is of the great things of Christ's nature, and I do not see how any one can be in doubt of the Bible feeling as to Christ. People may doubt whether they find any such statements as are in our creeds; namely, precise and logical statements as to the relation and equality of the Father, the Son, and the Spirit; but that the Bible is full of a great sense and impression of Christ every one can see. Even back in the Old Testament I see how full it is of some peculiar event, of some peculiar person, yet to come. I see that its sacrifices, its kingship, its prophets, seem to be a picture of something, of somebody, yet to come,— singular and wonderful, a far more wonderful sacrificial king and prophet.

In the New Testament I am astonished that any one can deny the apostles' sense of the singularity and divineness of Christ,— the very men who had seen and touched him. There is no description so high, no title so transcendent, which they do not frankly give him, lavishing an adoration which could not justly be given to a creature. But their sense of the height of Christ springs from their sense of the divine heart within him ; their sense of his natural elevation chiefly comes from their sense of his transcendent soul. They felt that " he had by inheritance obtained a more excellent name than they."

The revelation to them of the dignity of Christ came not from without but from within, — from their own inspired hearts. They saw a beauty which was fairer than the sons of men, fairer than any angels. In all his life — especially in his death — he, in words, in behavior, in feeling, in being, went not only up to, but far beyond, all they had known of God. They felt that this man had a higher, purer heart even than the dread Jehovah whom their fathers worshipped; his charm was such, so transcendent, so touching, especially in such moments as that when he said, " This is my blood of the New Testament which is shed for you."

Their souls were thus literally ravished; they loved, they worshipped, they said, " My Lord and my God."

They said it, not from the lips, not from the imagination, not from tradition or from creeds, but out of their whole soul. Nay, if their whole souls could have said anything higher, they would have said it, for conception could not set forth any rank too high for Christ. Before him, they and all beings cast down their crowns upon the ground.

There is in the Old Testament and in the New a vast array of evidence on the subject of the natural divinity of Christ. Long arguments may be made to the head, and we may consent, and say, "Christ is the second person of the Trinity;" but what is that to us? Something, no doubt. But only when we see Jesus Christ, when we feel that all external elevation, even of a natural Godhead, all the power, even of Almightiness, is nothing to the Godhead of his soul, of his human life on earth; only when we bow our whole self in adoration of that, in gratitude, in unbounded love to him who "was made so much better than the angels," who was made so through his love, through his cost, through his blood, emerging like heavenly gold through much tribulation, and who leads our hearts up after him into his high places, — not until we feel that, whatever else is high, or is called God, this head crowned with bloody thorns, this King of unspeakable self-sacrifice, is and can be nothing else than the highest, "My Lord and my God."

That was the apostles' orthodoxy, and doctrine of the Trinity. Man worships everything but the right thing. Even when he has the right God, he finds out the lower parts about him and worships these. He worships, for example, divine knowledge or power, or he worships a great natural Being, the God who creates, who sits on an almighty throne and wields the elements. But the God of gods is the spirit that was in Christ Jesus, — the spirit of mercy and of self-forgetfulness. One who reaches out, rescues, uplifts the world, not easily, but at his own cost, through his own blood; and if Christ be not that God, where is he? We have no such evidence that the God we see in Nature and reason is so high a spirit, so fine in heart, as the Christ of the New Testament is seen to be. The spirit that was in Christ is identical and at all points one with the very highest conceivable.

Let us make our creed begin by appreciating him! All belief will develop grandly out of that. When we learn to adore the Spirit, it will lead us into everything that is true. If we feel rightly there, we will think rightly as to everything in religion; for we will know him whom to know aright is truth eternal and life eternal.

XI.

THE FEAST OF EPIPHANY.

A light to lighten the Gentiles. — LUKE ii. 32.

AN Epiphany is a showing of something, a setting forth, a manifestation. Our Epiphany is the setting forth, or showing, of Christ to the Gentiles. This is a signal event, and worthy of our attention. It took place after the resurrection of Christ, and chiefly through the agency of Paul. It was beautifully foreshadowed, however, in an event which for poetical grace and sweetness is not surpassed by anything in the Scriptures, — I mean the worshipping of the Magi. "Now when Jesus was born in Bethlehem of Judea, came wise men from the east to Jerusalem, saying, Where is he that is born King of the Jews? for we have seen his star in the east, and have come to worship him."

This burning star in the far east, far out of the land of Judea, and the Gentile sages kneeling before the young child with their gifts, and gold, and frankincense, is the first Epiphanas of Christ to the nations, and exhibited, as in a splendid symbol, the greater manifestation that was soon to come. There seems a meaning in the fact that this took place at his birth, as if men were called to take notice that the child was intended from the first as a gift to the world.

This first showing of Christ to Gentiles seems to many to stand merely as a charming incident in the narrative of Jesus; but it was, in fact, meant to show from the beginning that Christ was for the whole race, not for any section of it; and thus to relieve, if I may so say, that strict, stern Judaism which in many respects he maintained during his life. He distinctly avowed that he was not sent, but to the Jews; and there were very important reasons for this; yet if there had been nothing to break its force, it would not only have fixed the minds of his followers yet deeper in their narrowness, but also it might afterwards have been objected that the extension of the religion to the Gentiles was an afterthought, and not in the original design. How finely wise, then, as well as beautiful, was it, to place this catholic fact and splendid prophecy — for such it was — at the beginning of his history!

We come now to the real and great Epiphany of Christ. After his ascension, his religion was opened to all mankind, — the everlasting doors of Truth set wide apart. This was a signal event, and remarkable on many accounts, especially to the great mass of the first disciples, who were Jews. I suppose that if the apostles had been asked, they would have placed this event among the most wonderful ever known.

They speak of it in language which astonishes us. Saint Paul calls it a mystery, — "*the* mystery which in other ages was not made known to the sons of men, as it is now revealed unto his holy apostles and prophets by the Spirit; that the Gentiles should be fellow-heirs, and of the same body, and partakers of his promise in Christ." He calls it again a "mystery, which from the beginning of the world had been hid in God." So unexpected and so wonderful was it, that even after the apostles were enlightened by the especial power of the Spirit, and taught in the profoundest spiritual mysteries, this plain thing, so it seems to us, they could not comprehend, — that Christ was to be given to the Gentiles equally with them. Peter was not convinced until he saw the vision at Joppa, and I am inclined to think that *he* did not (and perhaps also other of the apostles) overcome entirely the Jewish feeling so long as he lived.

How much of the New Testament refers to this either in one form or another, and how vast were the difficulties in the way of religion on account of it! We must not think that the entire difficulty lay in offering Christ to the Gentiles at all (that was only the first point in a long series), but in preaching his religion to all people in the independent and absolute form in which we now find it, freed from all Jewish trammels. They reached this last point most slowly, and they seemed to look upon the whole matter with a wonder not less than they felt at the miracles, or prophecies, or inspiration, or any of the stupendous events of that period.

There was more than their prejudice to be overcome. That God should become equally related to all, that the Christ was to become equally the Saviour and King of all, that all the God-given institutions of Moses should become at least unnecessary and finally be abolished, — there was enough in this to shock and shake any heart, though entirely free from blamable prejudice.

We can easily see that such a change as this would at first appear unreasonable, nor can we wonder at their feelings and conduct. They were indeed "slow of heart," as their Master said; but taking human nature as it usually is, these men were striking monuments of the power of God's Spirit, as in other things so also in this; namely, the extent to which the deepest and most nurtured prejudices were overcome.

The perpetuity of the old system seemed not only implied in the pains and cost with which it had been built up, but in the very fact that God had reared it. Can that be imperfect which he has established? Shall he pull down that which he has built? Besides, the old sacred writings are full of expressions as to the perpetuity of Zion, of which we now indeed can understand the deep spiritual meaning, but which they understood only of their own sacred city and temple and ritual. The manifestation, therefore, of the absolutely catholic character of Christ and his religion, and the setting aside of all that was local or temporary must have been a terrific change, — almost enough to destroy their faith. Their delays therefore were not wonderful; but I think there has not been so fine an instance of speedy emancipation from deep habit and deep belief since the world began.

There was not a view or a feeling of the Jewish mind, there was not a trait of the Jewish character, there was not an interest or a hope which was not against the showing of Christ to the Gentiles, against making *their* Messiah the Messiah equally of all the world. Their souls were against all this; therefore it is not wonderful that they opposed, but most wonderful to see how their hearts yielded, to see how *soon* those close, partial, intense Jewish souls were made unselfish, made so full of love, made so full of wide and noble thoughts, as to tear down the great wall of partition, to throw open with their own hands the gates of the Temple.

This was a remarkable event, not only as it chanced to oppose the prejudices of a particular people, but as being in reality a great and unexpected change in the divine dispensations; for though there were abundant intimations, such as those quoted in the Epistle to the Hebrews, that the Gentiles were in some sense to be brought in, yet not in such sense as the fact proved to be, — that is, not as fellow-heirs of the promise. *That*, at least, was never stated with such distinctness as to be anticipated, or Saint Paul would not have said that it was a "mystery hid in God." There were, I say, many such expressions as those of Isaiah: "The Gentiles shall come to thy light, and kings to the brightness of thy rising. . . . The abundance of the sea shall be converted unto thee, the forces of the Gentiles shall come unto thee. . . . The sons of strangers shall build up thy walls. . . . Thy gates shall be open continually; that men may bring unto thee the forces of the Gentiles, and that their kings may be brought." I do not, however, see anything in the real force of these expressions, or others of a like nature, which would give ground to anticipate any era when all men should stand alike before God.

Hitherto the divine Being had confined his revelations to a peculiar race; he now was to appear as the Father of mankind. The Epiphany of Christ to the nations was as if the public reassertion of the great fact that God was the Father, and sought to be the Redeemer, of mankind. This was a great change, a great advance in the divine proceedings towards men. This was one, and the most signal, of those great changes which occur in God's dealings with the race. At the very moment that religion became fit for all men, that was the moment when it began to be given to all. Whatever may have been the mysterious reasons which kept revelation within a certain limit before this, the great and perfect gift of his own Son he did not confine to any people. The work was no sooner completed, than the Spirit of God fell on Jew and Greek and Barbarian. He who was given for a light to the people was held up in all lands, spoken of in all tongues. The veil was removed which covered the face of the people, and the only-begotten of God, shining in peace and truth, was offered, to be seen of all.

Under the old plan the truth was fenced in; restriction after restriction was added, the people were isolated in various and wonderful ways from their fellow-men. But at the Epiphany of Christ began a great change in God's method: then rose an era, not of limiting, but of extending and expanding; not of hiding, but of manifestation; not of binding, but loosing. Contrast Saul of Tarsus, the scrupulous disciple of Moses, and a representative of the old era, — Saul, who would not fail in one iota of ritual or custom if the heavens fell; who would regard with unspeakable detestation the thought of giving up anything for the sake of a proselyte, — contrast him with Paul, who yielded everything, became "all things to all men," gave up so much that many thought he was no better than an infidel, simply because he would allow nothing that could be put aside to stand in the way of expanding the knowledge of the true God as he was seen in the face of Jesus Christ. Though Christ were preached of contention and strife, still, if Christ were preached, he gloried and would glory. To the Jew he was as if a Jew; at Rome, he was as if of Rome. The rule was, Christ must be shown; whatever stands in the way of that, though it were in itself good, becomes evil, and must be trodden under foot. The Epiphany of Christ has come; he must be set forth.

This is the contrast of the two eras. Epiphany — manifestation, a setting and diffusing forth — may be said to be the very name of the present era in God's Church. This has been the principle of his proceedings for eighteen hundred years. Whatever delays his providence has allowed, the Epiphany of Christ is still its one aim, steadily pursued.

When the Church in its corruptions obscured him, the Reformation gave him again a glorious manifestation. Forward through the future there await the world new and far more grand epochs of the same character, until the great and final Epiphanas, when no man shall say to his neighbor, "Know thou the Lord," for all shall know him, from the least unto the greatest; "When his throne shall be set, as the sun in the heavens, and every knee shall bow before him, and every tongue confess."

Let me now remark that if it be true, as I have said, that this is an era of Epiphany, and that to this great and overbearing purpose minor ones yield, — if it be true, I say, it is an important thought. If the Church had attended sufficiently to this one fact, there never would have been such a thing as a sect known in the world. If the attention had been intensely turned to showing Christ without scruple, if so be that Christ were shown, then, I say, the Spirit of love and wisdom would have filled all hearts into which the blessed vision came, and every minor truth, while it seemed to be neglected, would in fact be in the best manner conserved. Wise aggression is true conservatism, — that deep lesson the Church has yet to learn.

Let the few great central truths of the faith be borne inward on the heart, and that once well done, that aggression made, there will be time enough and will enough, and the right spirit then, to attend to and preserve all the minor portions of the body of truth. To show Christ, by which I always mean, to show the great features of his religion, is then the first great duty of all Christians, whether they would preserve or extend Christianity.

We have now seen that the Epiphany is a remarkable event, — more remarkable that among Jews the project should have been set on foot of giving their religion, their Messiah, on equal terms to all men, and that such a project should have been carried into effect by men to whom, in its conception, it was a thought absurd, and hateful beyond all expression.

The event was also remarkable because it was an unexpected and great change in the dispensations of God, making from that moment the strongest expansion and aggression the vital principle of his Church. It was a signal epoch in other particulars. At the very time that the Messiah was given as a "light to the Gentiles," he was as if withdrawn from his own kindred, and that people, hitherto elevated to heaven in privilege, were now thrust down, and the "nation scattered" with a vengeance such as had never been known on the earth.

But though the Messiah is now ours, it seems plain from the Scriptures, that he shall not be hid forever from them. " Though blindness in part is happened unto Israel, this is only to be [Saint Paul plainly says] until the fulness of the Gentiles be brought in." And then, " all Israel shall be saved." Not only, it appears, are they to be rescued, but it would seem that they are yet to hold some prominent place in the kingdom of Christ. For the same apostle reasons, if " the casting away of them be the reconciling of the world, what shall the receiving of them be, but life from the dead?"

Great as is the event of the Epiphany of the Son of God among us Gentiles, his future Epiphany among the Jews shall be (it would appear) a much more splendid and decisive event. " Behold, I have graven thee on the palms of my hands, and thy walls are continually before me!" And the great evangelical prophet Isaiah, alluding to the same event, says, " Whereas thou hast been forsaken and hated, so that no man went through thee, I will make thee an eternal excellency, a joy of many generations." " The sons also of them that afflicted thee shall come bending unto thee: . . . and they shall call thee the city of the Lord, the Zion of the Holy One." I would not say with too much assurance what all this may mean, but it is hard to give it any other meaning than that which is obvious, and on its front.

On this account this is an occasion on which the attention of the Church should always be turned with great interest to that wonderful people who, although they are yet a nation of outcasts, a by-word and a reproach, are awaiting perhaps a wonderful future. Or, if this should not be the case, what an affecting object of reflection should they be to us, for we are elevated on their ruins, and by their "impoverishing we are made rich."

We behold also in them what will certainly be true of us, however solid-seeming our civilization stands, — "The nation and the people that doth not obey God shall utterly perish, and their light shall be handed over to new people and races, fresh probationers in the great school of God."

With grateful and most humble hearts let us reflect on the giving of Christ to us Gentiles, that to us, "who sat in darkness, the light hath shined." Let us contemplate with awe both the severity and goodness of God, — severity to them whom he hath rejected, goodness to us whom he hath chosen and called. This the Church hath appointed as one of her highest festivals of gratitude. "Rejoice, O ye Gentiles; laud him, all ye people!"

XII.

THE CHARACTER OF CHRIST.

Blessed be the Lord God of Israel; for he hath visited and redeemed his people. — LUKE i. 68.

WHEN we commemorate the birth of any great person, a wide range of topics is opened to the mind. Whatever relates to him and has made his birth signal is matter appropriate to the occasion.

We usually, as one prominent topic, dwell upon the character of the person. We speak of his superior capacity, of his virtues, what evils he avoided, what good he realized, in what struggles he lived, how he bore himself; and beyond this we notice anything that may have been peculiar in the style of his excellence.

So, commemorating to-day the birth of Jesus Christ, it would be befitting to show, respecting his character at large, that in him dwelt all the fulness, both of wisdom and knowledge, and that he taught and spake as never man spake. All his words were aimed at the centre of things, so that in every fresh experience of life we are surprised to find his wisdom still taking us by the hand; and as it extends through all our experience now, and goes ever still before us, we may expect it will be so likewise through the higher stages of our existence hereafter. Many things we shall live past, — even knowledge shall vanish away, — new scenes, new faculties, new feelings shall arise; but the great central laws he has taught our childhood will go hand in hand with us through eternity, illuminating every new region we enter, and surprising us by a glory always new and always old. In this way might one speak of his wisdom.

Then, as to what is peculiarly called character, what might not be said of that? When on such occasions other persons are spoken of, the colors are usually somewhat heightened; but would one attempt to speak of the character of Christ, the aim must be, not to eulogize, but to do justice. The character of Jesus Christ! It is something quite alone, — a beauty, a grace, a depth altogether peculiar and sacred, as if there were but one star shining in the whole firmament.

His was a life lived out through the saddest history the world has on record, — lived sweetly out, — not deformed by his unheard-of sorrows, but made perfect by the things which he suffered. He was oppressed and afflicted, but as a sheep before her shearers is dumb, so opened he not his mouth. "When he was reviled, he reviled not again; when he suffered, he threatened not, but committed himself to him that judgeth righteously." There is an amazing excellence in the characters of some of the apostles; but the nature of Jesus has in it a peculiarity, a mystery of sweet holiness, appropriate only to him. He was "fairer than the sons of men." There is, it seems to me, that in his character which strongly resembles childhood, so that when our thoughts go back to contemplate the child of Mary there is something in our feelings very much the same as when we think of his nature at its maturity. He was in sweet innocency, in holy tenderness, in exquisite simplicity, always the child Jesus, the babe of Bethlehem. Some one, indeed, has called him the divine child, and, interpreted in this way, perhaps no description will give us a truer impression of him, the Lamb of God.

On the birthdays of great persons we also recall their achievements and lay them out before us. The great actions of Jesus Christ would afford scope for endless thought. His miracles, — behold them! He held the secret powers of Nature in his hand. Those ancient and unchanging laws, the awful and undisturbed order of God's works, he interrupted by a word. But higher things than these are among his works. He perfectly conquered himself; he lived perfectly his life. That was an achievement. He also so lived as to afford a complete model and example to humanity. That was an achievement. He presented in the truths he gave to the world, in what he did for the world, especially by his death, in the combination of light and motive he afforded to the heart of man, — he presented, I say, the opportunity, the means, the way, for the new birth of all things, for the re-establishment of all things on a new basis of glory and happiness as respects both time and eternity. So that when we commemorate the birth of Jesus we also commemorate the beginning of the new birth of the world and the great universe, — the palingenesia of things visible and invisible. This was an achievement.

When, years after the death of any great and good man, we assemble to honor his memory, we recount not only his acts but the effects of them; we trace the power of his influence on our affairs; we show the mark he has left upon the world. But what could a mortal tongue say of the influence of the birth of Christ upon the world? His spirit has penetrated into every department of human affairs, and has moulded everything it has touched. I will not ascribe to him all the melioration effected in the condition of man, — other causes have no doubt had their force; but this one cause stands incomparably above all others that can be named, and marks the beginning of the whole structure of modern civilization. It is all "built upon the foundation of the apostles and prophets, Jesus Christ himself being the chief cornerstone."

This wide world of commerce may not recognize him, but his power is felt at the very foundations of trade. This wide world of labor and art, in whatever form, owes its deepest obligation to his religion. That science which in these times has cast its intelligent and triumphant glance everywhere through the creation, — it may deny and cast out the name of Jesus, but to him, above the whole united catalogue of its lofty names, it owes its honors. Whence, also, this enlightened comity of nations which is making and going on to make of all the kingdoms but one great commonwealth, — can you tell me whence that comes? Or the widespread humanity which now marks the civilized part of the race, — whence is that?

In all departments of life there have been those who were illustrious for benefits conferred, and who deserve well of all posterity. Certain men have in certain things elevated the standard of the race, aroused some better feeling, or struck out some better view, which has become a possession to the world forever. Some have reformed a principle of government, and given a larger liberty to men. Some have stood forth nobly in defence of a human right. But we celebrate the birth of one whose life was the head and fount of all benefit, who in all things shows humanity the way, who laid anew the very foundation-stones of all duty, of all right, of all improvement, who pointed upwards to the heights at which men should aim, taught the means to reach them, and communicated the impulse. Why, in the one thought, not only taught but planted in the human soul, of the brotherhood of all men, — in that one thought is the secret of progression.

It must be admitted that this truth, as well as all his other truths, has not advanced far in its effects upon the world. At this day we see rapidly in progress among nations and upon a grand scale, by men who believe in him and by men who disbelieve, that very idea of brotherhood which without Christ would never have entered into the convictions of mankind; but he has sent it down into their hearts, and it works and will work, turning and overturning, until a better order of the world is settled. I recognize, indeed, in the grand fundamental impulse given by Jesus Christ to the moral world something far beyond what is of man; I see in it the same fine and powerful hand which first gave a planet its motion and direction in the heavens.

On each of these topics might we dwell exclusively, and on each of them might be opened the grandest views. Nay, we might go far beyond these views, and rise to consider who, in fact, this Being is whose earthly life was so pre-eminent. I might speak of the lineage of Jesus Christ, — for the splendor of ancestry naturally lends something of its lustre to descendants, — and tell that he was of the royal house of David; or I might rise higher, and announce that God was his ancestor, that his origin dated beyond the birth of the firmament or the sun. God " possessed him in the beginning of his way, before his works of old. He was set up from everlasting, from the beginning, or ever the earth was. When there were no depths, he was brought forth; before the mountains were settled, or the hills, while as yet the earth was not made, nor the fields, nor the highest part of the dust of the world."

But all these magnificent topics I have now hardly done more than enumerate, and so dismiss them.

In all the darkness of our natural state, groping, like the blind for the wall, a veil hung down upon the future, and man ignorant of the destinies of his own soul, lo, "the dayspring from on high hath visited us, to give light to them that sit in darkness." We know we are ignorant; the wisdom of God is incarnated for us. Poor, feeble creatures, an angel, and more than an angel, hath descended from heaven to strengthen us. We are conscious that all is deeply wrong within,—we all have gone astray, we have committed iniquity, we have done wickedly; but the Deliverer has come from Sion, who shall turn away iniquity from Jacob. Oh the unspeakable depth of rejoicing, the divine comfort in this thought, — Jesus born to save his people from their sins! Many pains and sorrows are around us, and death is standing before and not far off from each of us; but Christ is born, and sorrow, we see, can for each of us be turned into a joy which the world or fortune cannot take away; and death itself is changed into a most glorious gate of hope and life. Yes, the death of a man, which to the mere eye of Nature is the most tragical of sights, may become more divinely calm, of more magnificent joy, of more magnificent hope, than the setting of a summer's sun, an orb enlarging and enriching as it sinks.

XIII.

WHO IS THE SON OF MAN?

Who do men say that I, the Son of man, am? He saith unto them, But who say ye that I am? And Simon Peter answered and said, Thou art the Christ, the Son of the living God. — MATT. xvi. 13, 15, 16.

THE general opinion as to Christ among the Jewish populace must have been high. First the question, Who do men say that I am? He sought to find what response, what echo, men gave back to him. While he inquires, he hints the answer, — "that I, the Son of man;" for this his favorite title is always used, I think, to express the lowness of his condition, and to hint its height.

But who say ye that I am? And Simon Peter answered and said, "Thou art the Christ, the Son of the living God." Thou art not only in some low sense the Messiah, but the "Son of the living God." The merit of this answer was great. It seems easy to us; but we see all the higher side of Christ, and only that.

The imagination is a creator, and creates for and against. Here, it was all against. The Christ was a man, — from some province. His relations were known. Simon was daily with him, wearing the same common clothing, eating the same food. The greatest multitudes followed Christ for the feeding, the curing, and not alone for the wonder. There was therefore in Peter a special appreciation of the person before him. John loved his Master; so all: I think even Judas. But to the question — all silent! But Peter said, "Thou art the Christ."

Now this in general is a very great merit. Next to the hero is the man who recognizes the hero. Next to the high poet who enters is the single voice which in the general silence bids him welcome. But this case is very much apart. To appreciate a style of merit near us is one thing; but what a taste for the true grandeur had this Galilean fisherman, to believe that this was the Son of God, the chosen flower of the Jewish race, — against all the Jewish imaginings, against all ideas of the grand and beautiful Messiah, — that he so felt, so penetrated to the inner divineness of the man Jesus, that in spite of everything his lips first uttered, "Thou art the Christ." To see the Son of the living God in that most impenetrable of all disguises, nearness, familiarity, and commonness, required an unusual eye, an unusual heart.

But what is more, note the time when he did it, and note the fulness, unstintedness of the acknowledgment. All the theology of the Christian Church, all that power in Christian history which sprang from the great ideas of Christ and salvation, were wrapped up in that one full burst. It seems like a similar burst of confidence from a similar spirit in far antiquity, — "I know that my Redeemer liveth."

You can judge then at once of the feeling of Christ! It overflows. Why? Humanly, in gratification at being understood, the delight of recognition; that the good heart should spontaneously find him out; that without leading the good heart should echo his own deep knowledge. But the delight of Christ was far above this. The kingdom of God and its King, put in the world in a very peculiar way, was to be believed in, received, not from its splendors and visible majesty, — this kingdom was not to be imposed on the imaginations or even forced on the convictions of the world. Its Prince came in the shape of a quiet, most unworldly man, to be accepted by the right heart as the Highest because he was simply the Best. When Christ came, the earth was to be tested, whether it could love, receive, and enthrone the good because of its goodness. If the human heart was incapable of this, it might be fit for another sort of Prince, but not for the Prince Christ. It was not only virtue, but a very peculiar and unpromising style of virtue, which was presented. And as man nowhere had ever been given to adoring virtue, even in those shapes where it was much more suited to him, would he adore this most divine but most alien Christ? This was the question.

It was answered in a measure in all those people who had begun to love and vaguely reverence him; but in the heart of Peter it was first answered full and clear, —

and this was, that the problem was solved, namely, that absolute, pure virtue, not tricked out and bespangled, borrowing no aid from a foolish imagination, — that this could be loved and adored; and not by the refined and thoughtful merely, but by the common heart of fishermen and such like! The peculiar spirit and design, then, of this most original project was confirmed; what was purely, severely spiritual could be adored, and could be adored by those for whom it was especially intended. The Lord saw, I think, as by a glimpse of lightning, that the heart of Peter prefigured the good and honest human heart everywhere; that such a kingdom as he proposed was feasible; that he himself was the fit king of the common, human heart when it was simple and pure; and so it was that, in a sort of rapture, he exclaimed, "Blessed art thou, Simon Bar-jona." He had not confided in the human heart in vain. He sees Peter step forth, and in him he sees the first of the long series who will confess unto death, "Thou art the Christ."

He recognized in such discernment the light of that divine Spirit which illuminates all the good, — "Flesh and blood hath not revealed it unto thee." This did not come from your mind, Peter, or from the ordinary imagination and heart of mortals; it came from a new and instructed spiritual taste which discerned my glory, as the musical ear knows the musical sound; it is a heaven-descended insight. The keenest eye of mere nature never, never could see it, — could not then, cannot now. People talk of Christ, and many lavish eulogy upon him; but no man can truly say that Jesus Christ is Lord, but by the Spirit of God. "The vulture's eye hath not seen it." It is seen only by a glance from the true heart.

Simon Peter, then, not only declared and proclaimed who the Christ was, but in doing that revealed his own heart, declared and proclaimed who he himself was, — that he was one of the sons of God, who was capable of knowing the true Son; that he, Peter, was the first spirit of the coming Church, whose characteristic was to be the discerning and adoring of Christ.

And so we are now prepared to understand those words of Christ which through the last sixteen centuries have been so terribly abused. The dialogue is this: "Who am I?" "Thou art the Christ." "And I say also unto thee that thou art Peter, and upon this rock I will build my church." That is, you have declared to me who I am, and this enables me to declare to you who you are, — Peter, a stone, a rock of foundation; that is, you have in you a spirit of such description, of such kinship to divine things, that it can be trusted. This spirit is a rock of assurance, on which I will build my Church. The great honor and dignity which Christ's words gave, were given to that spirit of faith which at that time spoke through Peter, and which Peter represented, — to him and his *spiritual* (not official) successors. I will build my Church on this Petrine spirit, on this rocky substance.

But this is far from all. Besides this, these words can only be adequately and reasonably explained as a personal promise to Peter, in spite of Protestants. They meant to say that personal dignity was given to him; that as he gave the first decided enthronement to Christ, he himself was forever to stand as the first foundation-stone of the Church. Many shall confess me, but forever it is unalterable that *thou* art the first.

The historical priority is always regarded as a matter of weight in the Bible. Men are there as important, not merely from what they do and are, but also from the place they hold in the series. So with Adam, Abraham, for example; the thing is natural. This priority is not small. Among ranks of honor of every sort, in science, literature, empire, the founders have ever been thought of especial dignity. The Protestant world, which has rightly deposed Saint Peter from his false place, has wrongfully deposed him from the place in which he actually stood in the early Church; namely, as being not only one of the three great apostles, with James and John, but intended to bear in the rule of the Church a certain prominency among the brethren, — a somewhat especial respect; and this, not only because of his age and energy, which made him a natural leader, but because, I suppose, of the position in which the Lord himself had placed him, — I mean, as the first who had clearly acknowledged him.

So far is but just. Nay, I would go farther than that. Not only was he first in time, but there was clearly recognized in Peter an eminency in the spirit, and qualities fitting him for a prime leadership in the Church; and while true to the spirit of his confession, and just in proportion as he was true to it, was the promise a personal one. The promise, I say, was personal, but not absolute; it was dependent entirely on the elevation he maintained, in that spirit in which he began. So long as Peter showed the same eminency over all mankind as he did at that moment, being in faith before all, Christ declares he is in rank before all. It was the faith, the love of Peter which gave the rank of Peter. In the natural world gifts and honors are awarded according to many rules, often for no reasons, or reasons very arbitrary and partial; but in the spiritual kingdom all God's favors have but one base, — the measure of spirit. No partialities. So long as Peter remained highest in this spirit he was the natural Primate in Christ's kingdom; but if Peter fell away into another spirit, or even if he grew inferior to other souls, if a Paul should appear, and spread and rule the Church with a finer spirit than Peter, and create it anew with grander thoughts — But why talk of this? It is obvious enough that it is a personal promise, but just as obvious that it was conditional.

Look at the facts. That it was personal is seen by the history; we see it was actually, personally fulfilled. That it was conditional is seen just as clearly. The Lord interprets it so for himself in this very passage. Read on: "From that time forth began Jesus to show unto his disciples how he must go unto Jerusalem, and suffer many things." Now, this was not at all Peter's view. So " Peter took him, and began to rebuke him: Be it far from thee, Lord. But he turned and said unto Peter, Get thee behind me, Satan; thou art an offence unto me: for thou savorest not the things which be of God, but those that be of men." No words more intense. It was as if an odor from the pit had shocked his sense: and so everywhere. He treats Peter, and teaches others to treat him, as high or low, an angel or Satan, just according to the spirit he showed. When he sees the right flash, he cries out, " This is the strength and glory of my Church; " when he sees the common soul, he cries out, " This is the Satan."

Moreover, that it was conditional is seen also in the actual history. We see Saint Peter riding in fine supremacy for a time, like Hesperus in the evening sky, until a greater luminary (I mean Saint Paul) ascends and rules the night.

But enough of this. And yet it is not a trifling matter. A whole Christian world, through a large part of the Christian Era, is built upon this sentence, — these few words the creating edict. And carried so far to-day, it is solemnly declared that the successor on Saint Peter's throne not only rules the Christian Church, but rules it with a divine fulness, an infallibility, which did not belong to Saint Peter himself.

I may say, in general, that these gospel narratives of Jesus Christ can never be interpreted with full truth until there rises up a soul who from such congeniality with this Being, with his most unique modes of feeling and thinking, is authorized to say what he means. The spirit of the Church at large has interpreted justly, I suppose, the essence of the gospel; but the full interpretation of Christ is yet to come,— in the highest Church of the future, in some highest heart of the future!

The last thing to which I would call attention is, that when he had rebuked Peter he turned and said to his disciples, "If any man will come after me, let him deny himself, and take up his cross, and follow me." Most impressive is the utterance of these words just here, at this moment. For an instant he had seen before him the heart of Peter, so that he was filled with feeling,—I might say, enraptured; but in one moment he saw the same spirit shrunk up at the mere look of humiliation. The deep self, which lies under us all, the comfortable self, the proud and ambitious self, came forth. Alas! Disappointment, shock,—yes, disgust, aversion; so, "If any man will come after me, let him deny himself."

No matter how glowing religious feeling, how clear religious insight, how courageous religious confession, the test is, can we stand the cold, hard, grating denial of self? Are we content to suffer something, to be thought a little less of? Look at Peter, slipping down from heaven to earth; and that is the picture of us all. But oh the reality of Jesus Christ!

Here, two beings side by side for one moment, seeming to be alike, both exulting in pure spirit. "Thou art the Christ," says one. "Thou art Peter,— a rock," says the other. But immediately the one who is the Master, the one whose destiny from his loftiness would seem to claim some exemption, turns, and speaks of his coming sufferings with no reluctance,— embraces them and bows his head to them; but the other, the servant, at the mere thought of cold reality, of mortification, shrivels up, and is nothing any more. The steadiness and reality of Jesus Christ, who knew and accepted the fact that in the denial of self was his life,— that his life was not outside of that, but in it and by it!

That is a hard thing to make up the mind to,— that in the denial, death of our lower nature, and by that, is the life of our eternal spirit. Hard,— but once deeply realized and accepted, there is a joy and "peace which passeth understanding." "I have a liking for tribulation," said Paul; and this divine Master, the Great Head of all self-denial, speaks often of his peace,— his peculiar peace. And he adds just here: "For whosoever will lose his life, shall save it." What is that?

He means that for the death we suffer when we mortify self we find even now another life,— that the great idea of final resurrection is rehearsed and anticipated in every moment's experience. Nay, that the more real resurrection of the two — the soul's resurrection — is that which is now taking place. By every suffering I willingly accept in resignation to God, or in love for my Master, Christ, my soul springs and blossoms in spiritual life. Awaking to righteous life to-day is the first step of awaking to everlasting life to-morrow! And the awakening of to-day is as real, and a far more sublime fact, than the awakening of the body from the dust of the earth hereafter!

The Lord gave his few friends, then, two great facts of religion: the first, the chilling, sobering fact is, "If any man will come after me, let him deny himself and take up his cross, and follow me;" the second, the exhilarating fact, that this denial of a self is in reality the gift of a self, this death is a hidden life, an exchange of a poor and mortal soul for a pure and everlasting soul. "He that loseth his life shall find it."

XIV.

THE SCRIBES AND PHARISEES.

For I say unto you, That except your righteousness shall exceed the righteousness of the scribes and Pharisees, ye shall in no case enter into the kingdom of heaven. — MATT. v. 20.

A BOLD speech, uttered in the midst of a people where the scribes and the Pharisees were the aristocracy and power! It seems very important, then, to ascertain what was this righteousness of the scribes and Pharisees, because there is here such a clear statement that our righteousness, to be worth anything, must be of a very different order from theirs. I speak of these Pharisees, whose character in every view deserves the attention of all thinking persons. It is an old and trite subject, but because it reaches so far down into principles it is ever new.

This sect was so powerful, its vices and errors were so great, and it had such peculiar weight with the Jewish people at that time, that the teaching of our Lord might almost be described as a protest against Pharisaism, and his religion as a doctrine anti-Pharisaic. The two stand opposed to each other, as form to life, show to reality, reason to faith, pretence to substance; and no one thing will give so much light to Christ's words as the full and constant knowledge of this fact, namely, that he lived among Pharisees, and that the grandest aspect of his life and teaching was as a protest against them.

Pharisaism was the most extensive, inveterate, and authoritative form of evil which surrounded our Lord; he not only taught directly against it, but even in his ordinary instructions he naturally and wisely spoke with a side-glance of opposition to it, — giving to his doctrines the poignancy of contrast, not only to sin in general, but to the peculiar form which it had then taken. In such teaching, for instance, as this, "He came not to call the righteous, but sinners to repentance," we recognize at once what was in his mind. In the only place where he is said to have rejoiced, it was because such as they were abased, and the humble exalted. "In that hour, Jesus rejoiced in spirit, and said, I thank thee, O Father, Lord of heaven and earth, that thou hast hid these things from the wise and prudent, and hast revealed them unto babes."

Indeed, if we once get a clear notion of how great and pernicious a fact Pharisaism was at that time, and then read the New Testament with this idea always before us, we shall find a new meaning and force given to it throughout.

What distinctly were the Pharisees, and what was their character? They were the most powerful sect among the Jews, who had joined to God's law a vast body of minute additions, partly derived from traditions and partly from the authoritative interpretations of their doctors, and whose pride it was to believe implicitly, and to obey to a point and through all its endless detail, their vast and Brahminical system of religious observance. While they tithed " the mint, and anise, and cummin, they forgot the weightier matters of the law." The heart of religion, faith and feeling, was eaten out; they made their whole duty to consist in their trifling forms.

Now, if we wish to realize their characters, let us get clearly before us the idea of a man who by abusing his conscience has come conscientiously to feel that his whole duty, safety, and perfection are secured by certain outward rites and observances, and whose heart is then left free to be just what it may, with not one check of conscience; nay, his conscience indorsing and authorizing whatever he sees fit to do. For, feeling that he is entitled to the peculiar favor of God, and looked on with reverence and wonder by the people, and placed over their heads in Moses' seat, representing his awful religious authority, all the sanctions of religion are lent to give their power to his delusion. Man usually is only wicked against his conscience and every higher impulse; but this class of men feel they have all heaven on their side, let them be whatever they see fit.

This is a most wonderful condition of the human heart, and not rare; the likeness of it has often been repeated in the history of the world. There is no wickedness once to be named with this; for here that angel of light, the conscience, which dwells in the soul of every man, is no longer left as an accusing or reproaching spirit. Uncrowned and deposed, it lingers still in the confines of the heart, but becomes transfigured into an angel of darkness, and sits in the very seat made vacant by the delegate of God, and issues with the authority of heaven the very laws and liberties of hell! Church wickedness this is; and Church wickedness then, or at any time, is wickedness which has conscience to back it, or rather which by some legerdemain has introduced a disguised devil in the form of the conscience, and given to it the regal seat of the soul. No delusion can be conceived more hopeless or more malignant than this; and this was the state of the great Pharisaic body in the time of our Saviour. The poor people, awed, as they usually are, by a false show of sanctity, blindly followed their blind leaders.

You can see now the reason of the peculiar tone in which Christ speaks of the Pharisees. He speaks of this form of wickedness as he speaks of nothing else. He rises to terrible, blasting denunciation as he speaks of them. He withers them with a sort of solemn satire. He calls off the multitude from following them, and though standing in the midst of the land as the recognized aristocracy of righteousness, he points the finger at them, and with sublime courage proclaims, "Woe unto you, scribes and Pharisees, hypocrites! Woe unto you, blind guides! Woe unto you!"

It may seem strange, but I hesitate not to assert that the Pharisees are not dead, have never been, and never will be. This is a character which, with many modifications, belongs to human nature whenever it endeavors to give to its corruptions the sanctity of religion. As there are many reasons why the spirit of man, though merely worldly, does not choose or does not dare to cast off the advantages, or even the obligations, of religion, there is a necessity that it should work out for itself such a union with religion as will allow, under sanctimonious appearances, the indulgence of the corrupt realities. Conscious and entire hypocrisy cannot effect this result half so well, and is not half so agreeable to man, as where he can unite the complacency of a satisfied conscience with the inner wickedness of the heart. In no way can he do this so well as by demanding of himself an immense number of outward observances and austere self-sacrifices. For these hardships purchase his own applause, win over his conscience into proud satisfaction, and allow him, while he fulfils punctually his duty in nothings, to omit it in things of weight. Henceforth the man can believe he serves God even while he gives himself wholly to corruption. Here is the whole account of this strange condition.

It must be obvious to any one who knows the least of the history of his race or of the human heart, that in the ambiguity of all false religions, and nearly equally so in respect to the one true, divine faith, there are two grand evils, always present, always to be watched, — disbelief on *that* hand, formalistic hypocrisy on *this*.

These two have, in fact, one common origin, but taking different directions. With infidelity I have nothing now to do, though it is a greater foe than we know, and has many forms, and works while we sleep; but some form of simulated religion is all about us. All that we see in any and every church, and in any and every heart, which is not infidelity strictly, yet which is not love and trust in a merciful salvation, reverence to God, and affectionate obedience to his rules, with an earnest humanity towards the world of men, especially to those in whom shines the divine likeness, — all which is not this is of the nature of the "righteousness of the scribes and Pharisees," which, if we exceed not, we "shall in no wise enter into the kingdom of heaven."

I see in some churches the attention and also the heart concentrated and almost merged sometimes in doling questions of church government, and strifes of words; sometimes in questions of some real importance, as to who ought to be the rulers, or as to the order and character of the public worship in the churches, or as to the dogmas of religion, — discriminating nicely and laboriously, and working with all energy to set up a system of opinions in the minds of men. I see others yet, engaged with like earnestness in church building, in enlarging bounds, and supporting and managing the whole mechanism. I see the whole engaged for the heathen. This, of course, is all well; but it is possible that this all may stand to us much in the same place that religious ceremony, and even "the phylacteries, enlarging the borders of the garment," stood to less enlightened people.

Men feel that if they are doing something which is clearly of good result, or which may be so, if they make sacrifices or labor for that which is about religion, or which perhaps they persuade themselves is most important to it, — that if they are actually thus engaged, things are going very well. Sometimes the affairs of the heart indeed are slightly attended to, but soon slurred over, and the man is absorbed again, so far as his religious hours are concerned, in the things of which I have spoken.

Perhaps this is a picture of much of the religious life of the day; and perhaps it is true, as I have intimated, that man has still his way of living the life of the world even in the midst of the golden candlestick; his righteousness, all things being considered, not very far exceeding the "righteousness of the scribes and Pharisees."

The interval between this species of religion and the true is broad and deep as a gulf. Is religion a thing of the heart? Is it love, joy, peace in the Holy Ghost? Do we count attendance at church, activity in church affairs, the act of communing, a ready liberality, as *nothing* unless they proceed from a living principle of love, God-ward and man-ward? Yet further, may we not have a sort of religious faith, be interested in the truth and ready to defend it, — and in many matters this faith may regulate our lives, especially in the outward framework of them, — yet all this may not be essentially different from what our Saviour calls hypocrisy?

No one can state this so strongly as Paul does: "Though I have all faith, so that I could remove mountains." What power of religious belief! "Though I bestow all my goods to feed the poor, and though I give my body to be burned, and have not charity," — that is, though I have all the outside and not the inside, — I am nothing. Here is the core and vital centre of the whole matter, — love; and if that be not in the heart, though everything else be there, though all wear so fair an appearance that neither the eye of man nor spirit can find any flaw, — yet before God who knows the heart we are but as the sound of the empty brass and the noisy tinkle of a cymbal. But let nothing now said discourage; for it is incomparably easier to be the real thing than to be the false.

Nature builds her plants, animals, and all her living structures from within outwards. The beautiful soul or principle of life from which she begins, works out and through the fair structure of stem and leaf and blossom and fruit. The life of a Christian must be built in the same manner, from a great, all-shaping principle of gratitude, — *love*, — which shall make all his external acts not only symmetrical, but full of life; not an empty form, built around the soul of the man, not "the righteousness of Pharisees," — not the form of a dead man, which, though perfect in every part, the machinery of the heart all in order, has no heart-power, no stream of vitality poured through the system, no warmth in the flesh, no color in the skin, no life in the eye.

I call all to a vital religion. In that only is there joy and power. "Make clean the inside of the cup and the platter." Cleanse out the bones which lie within the whited sepulchre of our daily lives. Away with religious ostentation, which loves the prayer in the market-place, — with religious ambition, which would seat itself in the chief rooms, — with religious benevolence, which sounds its trumpet before, — with the blasphemous religious pride, which dares in the presence of God to feel that we are not as this publican; away with religious worships and sacrifices and hard duties, while we have such hearts within us! O holy name of religion, defied, abused, defamed! All these things are an "abomination to me, saith the Lord."

XV.

THE JUDGMENT.

When the Son of man shall come in his glory, and all the holy angels with him, then shall he sit upon the throne of his glory, and before him shall be gathered all nations, etc.— MATT. xxv. 31-46.

A PICTURE of judgment. Who is the Judge? The Son of man. Especial emphasis is given to the fact that he is to be the Judge of the world. "For the Father judgeth no man, but hath committed all judgment unto the Son." A broad commission! And the Son of man claims to be worthy. "If I judge, my judgment is true." And the reason given is his humanity. Here is the express announcement. "The Father hath given him authority to execute judgment also, because he is the Son of man." I do not know any fact more striking. As "judgment" means to test, to reveal, and as the light tests or reveals the darkness, so the perfect human glory of Christ expresses the true character of all other men, and thus judges them. He is, then, not merely the Judge by office and at some coming time, but he is by what he is, essentially the test of men.

Is not every noble person as he stands before our eyes a silent reprover of the base and an approver of the noble? Does not the statue of the Apollo detect and condemn the common ugliness, and countenance the fair proportions which are akin to itself? So Christ, and even while on earth and though men saw him with eyes stupid and bleared by sin and sinful prejudices, yet enough was seen to attract and bring out the good heart and expose the bad. "For judgment," he says, "I am come into this world." Not that he desired or designed to condemn the world ("I came not to condemn; I came not to judge," as he frequently declares); but the testing, the judgment of which I speak, was an indisputable fact of his presence.

And this judgment of the world has gone on increasingly since. The more Christ is known, the more utterly the false ideals, the falsely splendid characteristics, and all the meanness and sin of the earth are shown and put to shame. He stands as the measure and standard of all the generations as they pass by him; as the one lawgiver, so also the one perpetual Judge.

And when the world beholds Christ truly ("and every eye shall see him"), the full sight of that life of his, lived out in circumstances no better than ours, lived out in streets and houses certainly no better than these, lived out in an experience no less trying certainly than our experience, — that glory of humanity, forged in the same workshop where we work, will exhibit in full daylight the possibilities of humanity, and fathom the depth of the fault in all our race. Beyond this, he shows what we are, not merely by what he is in general, but by what he is to us. When the world comes to see him as its redeemer, as one who aimed to rescue and uplift it by such cost and sacrifice to himself, the fairest image creation ever beheld offering himself to us and for us, will he not, if he is once seen crowned with thorns and with the blood upon his body, show us what is the blackness of our cold rejection of him; tell us and tell the universe just what manner of souls we are, and so, and by no arbitrary decision, assign us our place?

But it is his direct and official judgment which is now properly before us. And as to that I assert that there is not in the Bible a more profound and beautiful fact than the selection of the Son of man for the Judge of men. Is a mere man fit? An angel? God? Neither. No man, no angel: nay, nor God himself. For the purposes of this high justice to come demand not merely that there shall be justice administered, but that it seems (to us and to all) to be justice; the clearness and impressiveness of the justice is a prime point.

Though God himself is an infinitely just Judge, is the anticipation of his judgment by such a race as ours as clear and salutary to our minds as when we anticipate a judgment by the Son of man? If an invisible and incomprehensible Being is to judge us, "whose thoughts are not your thoughts, neither are your ways my ways," people will either think of him with a blind dread if he is supposed to be just, or a blind assurance and ease if he is supposed to be a God of love. So on the one hand whole generations of men formerly turned God into a monster of vengeance, and the whole world groaned under a mere brute fear, and so latterly masses of people turn him into a monster of easiness. As to a Being so vague to us as God is, of whom we are so ignorant, if the human mind takes one direction, say as to severity, there is nothing to limit it, our fears drive us on, and he becomes to our eyes implacable; and on the other hand, if we take the other turn, he becomes so placable that he ceases to be a moral Being at all.

But as to the Son of man, it is impossible from ignorance to run into these extremes; we know his heart, I think, better. We have seen him and touched him, and we know how solemn the depth of sin is to him; that he must ever turn away from it and condemn it, we see by the blood upon the cross, its nature and its results. We see by what he was — one unspeakably "separate from sinners" — that there must be an everlasting banishment of sin, yet we see as distinctly a mercy which will reach us and forgive us so long as we can be reached and forgiven; that while there is one spot of life in the soul, one redeemable centre, one wish for purity, one longing to obey, aught akin to truth and Christ, so long that Judge will not irredeemably cast out; so that when he does cast out, when the face of Jesus Christ is turned from any creature, when the wrath of the Lamb begins to burn, love itself approves of the justice, and we know that the soul is only fit to be cast out upon the refuse-heap of the universe.

Here, then, is just what is needed and all that is needed in the Judge of the human race. Think of Christ for one moment as not divine; think of him only as the purest, wisest, most suffering, and most generous of the sons of men, — that he, such an one, our own brother, should be placed on the throne of judgment to judge us, is the most consolatory of facts. How pitiful and gracious to us that God should place him there! How sure we are of all consideration from him, of all mercy that is mercy! and yet no false indulgence, no immoral weakness, for he is also the Son of God, calm and holy, of "purer eyes than to behold iniquity," and whose justice when it must come penetrates the heart like a sword because it is rendered in sorrow, because he is one who weeps over the city he is about to destroy.

If, then, he condemns me, it is a divine condemnation; and yet he will not condemn me if he can save me. The Judge as he sits there is also the Saviour, the same heart; redemption is his aim, judgment only the necessity, and if this be a redeemable spirit of mine he will be sure to find it out, and though he give me the lowest place, so that it scarce seems heaven, still I shall stand far distant but within the circle of the saved! With these views, I think the sight of the future judgment-seat of the Son of man a sight which more inwardly and touchingly " reforms me of sin, of righteousness, and of judgment" than any other sight, if I except the sight of his cross! It was fit, then, that the Father should give him authority to execute judgment also, because he is the Son of man.

As to the circumstances of that judgment, perhaps there is nothing in all which the genius of man has produced, equal in impressiveness to the scriptural descriptions of judgment. They are numerous and various; some of them more simple, some more splendid, but all of a wonderful moral sublimity. One from the twentieth chapter of Revelation, "And I saw a great white throne, and him that sat on it, from whose face the earth and the heaven fled away; . . . and I saw the dead, small and great, stand before God; and the books were opened; . . . and they were judged every man according to their works." This is one picture of that great transaction. In the text we have another, in the simple, almost homely manner of the Son of man; and yet it seems to me, if possible, more wonderful than the other. All such representations are merely accommodations to the human mind. But if we consider that great event (whether gradual or on some one day, whether public or private) merely as a matter of the soul in the presence of its Maker, that is enough. Once illuminate the spirit with a sense of the holiness which condemns, or of the mercy which saves, and all outward strength becomes nothing. Or take these awful descriptions and reverse the circumstances. Instead of the noise and commotion of the gathering of men and of nations, let there be simply silence, — the solitude of the soul with itself and its Judge; instead of the flashings of justice like lightnings from the east to the west, let there be but the clear sight of facts, and we have the Judgment!

The Test. What is it? "I was an hungered, and ye gave me meat: I was thirsty, and ye gave me drink: I was a stranger, and ye took me in: naked, and ye clothed me: I was sick, and ye visited me: I was in prison, and ye came unto me,"—that is, as it is explained, "inasmuch as ye have done it unto one of the least of these my brethren, ye have done it unto me." The spirit, then, which is made the test of judgment, is what? Does it mean general humanity to man? for all men are his brethren. I think it does not exclude that meaning, but that it means primarily and emphatically sympathy towards those who are like him, not necessarily for the sake of him, for it seems they were ignorant of any reference to him in the transaction. "When saw we thee an hungered, or athirst, or a stranger, or naked, or sick, or in prison, and did not minister unto thee?" The spirit so highly approved, then, so far as I can discriminate, is appreciation of and sympathy for truly right people, especially when in distress. I do not say for Christian people, for that is confusing: so many Christians so called—yes, quite prominent and standard Christians—being little or not at all in the true spirit of Christ; and, on the other hand, some I think who have never heard of Christ, and many who for a thousand reasons never formally call Christ Lord, being still in some real sense his, — his genuine brother at the heart. Now, love of such, succoring such, is a certain test that we are of such; for our appreciation of others always reveals what we are.

Once discover what a man's admirations and disgusts are, and you measure exactly what he is. If he instinctively turns to whatever is popular and prosperous, and regards the surface only, he is a man of the surface; if he instinctively bows and is loyal to the true man and the true thing, no matter how unpromising it all looks, nay, all the more if it be distressed and outcast, if he is disgusted, not at all with bad fortune, but only with the mean heart; if he admires and his heart rises to any show of the pure and beautiful and heavenly tempers of Christ; if he recognizes what is really high and what is really low, and comes forward to take up the truth when it is a stranger or in prison, — that man has the approval of the final Judge.

The man who has this spirit, though he be ignorant, though unfortunate obstructions keep him away, has yet the seed of the kingdom within him, and will gradually and in better circumstances come forward to all essential truth with the same certainty that the plant in a cell of darkness sends out its shoots to the light. His foundation is of gold, and will stand when the wood and hay and stubble be burned. Yes, the word to him is, "Come;" while to another, covered over perhaps with correct doctrine, and saying, "Lord, Lord," but who has no heart in his bosom, — to that other the word is, "Depart!" It is very strange that this great test should at this day be made so little of.

Common humanity — humanity to man as human — is coming to be with the world at large the only test I think very much of this spirit of humanity when pure and not politic; it is one of the best of the fruits of Christ. Certainly it is a far better test, and will stand the fire far better than many of the accepted tests. But this stream cut off from the fountain in which it originated — humanity apart from Christ — I am afraid will soon run impure and more impure, and will at last dry up. And certain I am that while Christ may be said to be the author of, and while Christianity lives at the base of, this common humanity, yet the thing which has his special approval is far higher than that; it is sympathy, not merely with man, but with those who are like him, — humanity to the sons of God. The gospel is no leveller of men, as this age aims to make it. Nowhere do I find such a deep discrimination, such a deliberate and marked selection of a class, — the class of the truly noble. Christ chooses them, sets them up, and makes our own characters to be tried by the love and homage we pay them. This seems now to be forgotten. Let us awake to it.

Where I see the spirit of Christ, let me deeply bow down to it. Where I see a man doing right at a sacrifice, steady under trials, unselfish, nay, forgetful of self, wronging no man, and magnanimous when he is wronged; just, just even to his enemy; merciful of heart; uninflated with absurd vanities and foolish self-estimations; despising shows and unawed by public opinion; a man who, when other men think it Christian to compromise and keep quiet and side with the strong is then only more terrible and inextinguishable against wrong; a man who with all this is grateful and humble and resigned to his Maker, and above all who turns with an unspeakable adoration to Christ his Master, — this man, or any man who is but a sketch and rudiment of this, if I see him and do not know him, love him; if I see him " hungering " and give him no meat; if I see him in prison and come not unto him; when other men cast out his name, if I do not pronounce it, — then I am but a poor creature, call me what you will. Loving not the brother of Christ whom I have seen, I do not — how can I? — love and honor Christ whom I have not seen. By this ladder we ascend to God; loving his divine image in the creature as the reflection of stars in broken and turbid water, we rise to adore the direct effulgence of the heavenly lights.

It is affecting and beautiful that the Lord of all should give us so simple and easy a test of a right heart. He did not treat the human heart as many ancient and modern theologians have treated it, by laying heavy burdens upon it hard to be borne, making a thousand conditions, applying a thousand tests. He reduces religion, for our comfort, to a very simple thing, — loving them who are really like him; and we will succor them and be kind to them for the sake of him who succored us in our low estate.

Above all, let us pause a moment at the fact that he, the highest, makes himself absolutely one with his children. "I was hungry, and ye gave me meat; I was thirsty, and ye gave me drink," etc. He thirsts with the thirst of his meanest and lowest brother; he is in prison and a stranger with him. Therefore, lift up your heads, ye weakest strugglers after the true life, if your heart be right, for your Lord is so one with you that if you bleed he bleeds; and so precious are you, that the whole race, kings and princes, are to be judged by the heart they have towards such as you.

I have spoken of the Judge, the judgment, and one of the great tests of judgment. In that dread judgment we are all to stand; the face of that Judge we must behold; we near it daily; we shall stand before that great white throne, and one question we must all answer, — Did you love the Lord Christ; did you honor and succor him whenever you saw him (under whatever veils of poor humanity); did you hold out your hands to him and bear him up? If so, "Well done, good and faithful servant; enter thou into the joy of thy Lord."

XVI.

THE EXALTATION OF THE HEART.

Then came to him the mother of Zebedee's children, worshipping him, and desiring a certain thing of him, etc. — MATT. xx. 20-28.

THIS was just after the plaudits and high demonstrations which the festal caravans on their way to Jericho gave to Christ, and the minds of the disciples were naturally excited as to his coming greatness, and their part in it. He himself seemed to confirm their material conceptions. "Ye are they which have continued with me in my temptations, and I appoint unto you a kingdom," etc.

"And he said unto her, What wilt thou? She saith unto him, Grant that these my two sons may sit, the one on thy right hand, and the other on thy left, in thy kingdom." That is, they request that the first position of dignity and power may be theirs.

In justice, this was not entirely ambition. Remember who they were, — James and John. The best affections at once heightened and excused the selfish desire. So often our passions "take the livery of Heaven to serve the Devil in." Especially is it true, that (as to the mother) parental affection and household ties often in a thousand ways foster selfishness to those without, quite in contrast to the beautiful Roman tale of the mother of the Gracchi.

"But Jesus answered and said, Ye know not what ye ask." Ye know not what dignity it is; nor the way. Ye are not aware that, like the child which stretches towards the splendid blaze, ye are reaching out for a consuming fire. Nor (seeing that ye seek this as a personal favor) are ye aware of the fine laws of justice, which are my Father's will, and which assign each man his place apart from all favoritism or personal relations to me. So that rank "is not mine to give, but it shall be given to them for whom it is prepared of my Father." Ye know nothing of the whole.

But after this general assertion of their ignorance and folly, he being filled with a sense of the magnitude of his own coming sufferings, and knowing what that dignity they sought to share would cost them, seems to concentrate his surprise chiefly there, and asks, as if the question admitted of no reply, and would test and settle the whole matter, "Are ye able to drink of the cup that I shall drink of, and to be baptized with the baptism that I am baptized with? They say unto him, We are able."

An astonishing reply! False self-reliance is in religion, and even in life, weakness; while yet mighty things, at least in this world's affairs, are effected by "We are able." Yet even here, as Lord Bacon remarks, "A man is raised up and made more successful who feels himself in the care of the higher powers. Sylla chose the name of *Felix*, and not that of *Magnus;* and it hath been noted that those who ascribe openly too much to their own wisdom or policy commonly end unfortunate." It is written that Timotheus the Athenian, in giving a public account of his services to the State, having used the words, "and in this, fortune or the gods had no part," never prospered in anything he undertook afterwards. And we see ourselves that even the men most self-relying, and with a magnificent sense of personal power, such as Napoleon, where they had no other religion, sustained themselves by a deep confidence in a mysterious agent which they called Fate. Still, no one can deny that the feeling, "We are able," is often sublime when man combats with Nature or with man. When, however, his self-reliance is as to his virtue or religion, it is a shameful weakness compared to the power which comes into him through resting upon God. The same great writer, in his Essay on Atheism, has this fine passage: "To be without God destroys our power; for, take an example of a dog, and mark what generosity and courage he will put on when he finds himself maintained by a man, who is to him instead of a God, or higher nature. So man, when he resteth and assureth himself upon divine protection and favor, gathereth a force and faith which human nature in itself could not attain." And

I may add here that this resting upon what is divine, whether upon God as our author or upon God as our Saviour, is the eminent peculiarity of the gospel, — is that, in fact, which distinguishes it as a spiritual system, so that the gospel may be described in one word as God-reliance or Christ-reliance, not self-reliance.

Granting, then, that much of a weak self-confidence marked the answer of the sons of Zebedee, yet their spirit, though it needed chastening and humbling, was marked by a devotion which made all things seem possible to them. There was an affection and abandonment of *self*, under all their presumption, which endeared them to the Lord; for not the faultless people, coldly correct, are so prized by him as the warm though often foolish heart; as in the Old Testament, not any faultless model, but the warm-hearted David. Viewed on this side, we could wish no better wish for the Christian Church and all its members than such heartiness. "We can do all things," adding, however, "through Christ strengthening us."

So much for them. And now as to Him. At the first hearing of their request his feeling was simple amazement. There is observable in him a sense of the endless distance between him and them. You drink such a cup! Knowing them, and the little frail human heart in them; knowing the fathomless depth of his own sorrows and exigencies, the fathomless depth of the holy will, and the holy, filial trust that were in him, — so deep that the infinite of trial was met as if by a deeper infinite of submission and pure obedience, — comparing, I say, these poor, ignorant children of the earth, who thirsted to share his throne, with the character and awful history necessary to reach it, we can conceive the feeling, " Are *ye* able? "

But when they look up to him and say, in their presumptive but simple-hearted confidence, " We are able," a change like lightning seems to pass through his whole consciousness; he remembers that they too, in their measure, will indeed share his cup. They are poor, ignorant children; but then, they are his children, and he knows they will be faithful and affectionate unto death. And then he adds in a deep and tender tone, " Ye shall drink indeed of my cup, and be baptized with the baptism that I am baptized with," adding, however, that rank in his kingdom was not to be dispensed capriciously, or by personal favor, but according to his Father's will, — that will which was all justice and all insight, and on which rested all law.

Consider together the two expressions, " Can ye drink of the cup that I shall drink of ? " and, " Ye shall drink indeed of my cup." As I have already intimated, they mean much as if he had said, " I admit you shall share with me trials, in order to conquest, — that, indeed, is yours, — but I have a cup to drink that ye know not of; when I tread the wine-press alone, of the people there shall be none with me."

Now, here are indicated two of the greatest ideas of

Christianity, and which run all through it; namely, that we are as if one with the divine Lord, that "as he is, so are we in this world," and yet, that he transcends and passes out of our experience. On the one hand, that our cup is as his cup; and on the other hand, that our cup is not as his cup.

It is true that like him we are set forth to be purified through suffering, and that the history of every faithful man is the history of Jesus Christ over again. This is one of the most animating and uplifting truths of the gospel. But it is also true that in him there is a superhuman singularity of character, a transcendence, a privacy of work, of suffering, and of destiny.

There is a cup of which no man has drunk, "save him who once tasted of death for every man." And if this be true, then if any man claims to have himself drunk of that cup, and to have gone down into that mysterious baptism, — claims, "I am able," that is, that he is his own Saviour (and there are not a few of such in all churches), I have no quarrel with him further than to say that I regret he can spare a Saviour, as many of us feel we cannot, and that if we are to be the Saviours of ourselves, our hope goes out, and the very light in the heavens grows dark.

"And when the ten heard it, they were moved with indignation against the two brethren." I have no doubt they felt it a just and virtuous indignation, and so most people do who read the narrative. But here speak out, I think, envy and discontent, which are but reversed forms of the same ambition. "They were moved with indignation" that these two aspired above them, which in reality was the same spirit, though in less degree than that at which they were indignant. And so it is not uncommonly. Our dislikes and hatreds of other people — nay, even our most righteous indignations — are often against conduct which, with a little difference of shading, is just our own. We are engaged in pulling out the motes from other people's eyes, while the beam is in our own. And what a sight it must be to any vision which can see better than ours the proud assumptions, the intense contempt, the standing apart, like the Pharisee, when essentially the same low feelings are prevailing with all, the accuser as with the accused. "The ten were moved with indignation."

The Lord meets this anger, not indeed with rebuke, for he was sparing of rebuke, but by teaching that which, while it quieted their anger, laid the foundations of entirely better thoughts. "Jesus called them unto him, and said, Ye know that the princes of the Gentiles exercise dominion over them, and they that are great exercise authority upon them. But it shall not be so among you; but whosoever is great among you, let him be your minister, and whosoever will be chief among you, let him be your servant." That is, he allows the human ambition for excellence and elevation, but just changes the whole thing aimed for. Be ambitious, not to get, however, but to give; not to be lording, as the Gentiles, but ministering.

Aim for dignities, but the dignities of lowliness. Not the dignities of pride and selfishness, but the dignities which consist in generosity, and which will take the place of a servant if it can confer a benefit, rather than of a king to exact a service. "For [he concluded] even the Son of man came not to be ministered unto, but to minister, and to give his life a ransom for many." The kingship, even of the Highest, was not to sit down upon a throne, selfishly imposing his will on all beneath, but to stand, as the minister, servant, or even slave (as the word means), to stand as the mighty slave of Love; giving, giving, until he gave even himself— that is, his life — "a ransom for many." That is to be the style of the new kingdom.

In this little speech is the reversal of all the master-ideas of the race, their overthrow, down even to the roots. It is the far-off announcing of the final judgment of "contempt and hissing" upon the whole kingdom of selfishness, from its "turrets to its foundation-stone."

Having completed the narrative, I will dwell on two thoughts, — how greatness is to be reached, and what the greatness is.

Greatness is to be reached through tried character, by a soul formed in the *fires*. Ye sons of Zebedee, who seek to share my throne with me, do you know what it is to share that with me? It presupposes and demands a history and a character, a cup and a baptism. Can you share these with me? Exigency and sorrow are the stuff out of which the first Son worked his sonship to God; and so, after him and through him, must all other sons, even we. And from this, and this alone, all sitting upon thrones must come at last. The sonship of God is created, as all fine things are created, through opposition. All life, even up to soul, is created through what resists it. In the first and lowest appearance of life in Nature we see it forcing the hard substance of the rocks into moss and lichens, and making flowers out of flint. And so up to soul. This is the law.

But the last point I wish to fix attention upon is the nature of the greatness man is appointed to reach. Man is not nearly so different from the lower animals as Christ's idea of greatness is different from man's. His thoughts and feelings are those of a distinct order of being. Nay, not merely different, but precisely opposite. He turns the lower pole to the top. The dominion of me upon you, the superiority of me to you, — that is man's idea. "Ye know that the princes of the Gentiles exercise dominion over them, and they that are great exercise authority upon them [the idea is of a power above imposing its will upon what is below]. But it shall not be so among you." That is, your greatness consists in descending through love down from the throne to the ground, in yielding your will to the will of God and to the good of man; in emptying the soul of self, of its will, of its demands, and being, henceforth, not one that takes, but one that gives.

This, which is the most original and revolutionary thought the world has heard or can hear, was elicited, how? Why, just as we see that Christ's heavenly ideas were usually elicited, — by some folly or sin of the common men about him, as a glancing light struck out of some dark and passing cloud. Instead of God's coming forth from the cope of the sky, and with a great noise announcing his idea of greatness to the listening kings of the earth, these great words are spoken with quiet simplicity, on occasion of the foolish thoughts of two young fishermen and their mother, — words which have leavened and are leavening the lump of the world, moulding slowly, but moulding surely, the hearts of the human race, and drawing out, as by an almighty power, the very tap-root of all human delusions, drawing it as if out of the very bowels of the earth.

As to this great idea itself, kingship is service, and the first king is he who is most entirely a servant. That sounds disagreeably enough; but what is it? Merely that selfishness, however grand it makes itself to look, and however much spoil it has gathered around itself, and whatever the crowns it puts upon its head, is not the true king. But that disinterestedness is the true king, though it be deposed and covered with rags.

This, when it was taught, was the most original

thing ever uttered as a principle for the world. For the nations so far had even no sense that selfishness was sin, or disinterestedness was virtue. They had their vices and virtues, of course, but these were not among them. Yet these, according to their new Teacher, included all the rest.

Original and grand as this then was, it is hardly less so now. We have indeed grown up to a sense of the immorality of selfishness. We have some glimpse that Christian charity ascends above Roman and Greek virtue and Jewish duty; but until to-day these words, which make it identical with all loftiness, and its opposite selfishness identical with all baseness, — this fact, that it puts the poor laborer, who is in the spirit of Christ, on the highest throne, and puts down the most towering king from his seat, and puts him in the dust and ashes, this is yet far before us, though we admit it in words. We know not yet the meaning of Christ, but we shall know it hereafter, — nay, that this Christian disinterestedness (call it charity) included not only all old virtues, but quite a new region and sphere of virtues, which is to the old as heaven to earth.

What is the man but his soul, and what is the baseness of the soul but its selfishness, and what its dignity but its generosity? Is there anything detestable but selfishness in all its disgusting forms of pride, and vanity, and conceit, and mean ambition, and envies, and hates, and treacheries, and cruelties? Is that a king? Is not that a slave? And on the other hand, if we be above barbarians, is there anything worthy of our admiration and enthusiasm but the soul which has sunk self and glows in devotion to something else?

What is the Godhead of God himself but this spirit? The one King Eternal and Immortal, the one Lawgiver is himself *Love;* and he who appeared to show him to our eyes, appeared, not ministering to himself, but was in the form of a servant, and died in an act of service. And is it not true that so far as any creature approaches that, has received that spirit, so far he partakes of the kingliness of the Divine Nature? Yes, faithful to-day "in few things," his Lord one day will make him "ruler over many things."

These are laws, not fancies. "Know you not," says the great apostle, "that you shall judge angels?" He meant something. If we wished proof that disinterestedness is the secret beauty and secret elevation of heaven and of earth, the proof is that, we ourselves being judges, when we see it as it was in Jesus Christ, it stands forth evidently divine, even to us, and we cry out at once that God has been among us, and in some sense all men join in the cry.

Rejoice, then, in the soul which God has put within you. If you have in your heart but one gleam of Christ's pity, self-sacrifice, and munificence, rejoice in that, for that begins the kingdom of heaven. He who seizes the just view of the temper of the King of kings, he who delights in that, takes that as his portion, while he can believe and must believe that that spirit which God puts in him is the loftiest reality, the imperial fact, and that it is fit and prepared for any outward throne; yet he can believe this without disturbance, for in the reality he possesses he has lost the taste for vulgar shadows, and would put by all sceptres as playthings, unless through them he could better reach some high end of the heart. He can ever feel (as Jeremy Taylor writes) that "his crowns and sceptres spring from crosses;" that it is the cross which is the glory. As the cross stands wrought on the top of the globes and sceptres of earthly kings, and gives them all their glory, so much more of his. But however poorly we from our weakness may be able to combine the consciousness of lowliness with elevation, let us remember always that there stands before our eyes, for our imitation, a being who was at once and naturally "the meek and lowly," while yet wearing "on his head many crowns," whose consciousness of height did not impair his modesty, nor his lowliness check an unbounded sense of his dignity.

Be more like Christ, and then, in your consciousness of oneness with the pure and eternal spirit, in the consciousness of some share in that divine heart which loves and gives, and claims nothing, and which will go through Gethsemane or Calvary on its errands of mercy,—in that you will know that you are a son and heir of the Highest; and that there is but one *exaltation*, that of the heart.

XVII.

THE GODLIKENESS OF MAN.

So God created man in his own image, in the image of God created he him. — GEN. i. 27.

ALL the false religions and all the false practical ideals of the world are just the reversing of this. Those great ideas in the Bible that there is one perfect divine Being, God, and that man is formed in his image, and through all disasters is to be re-formed into that image, — these two ideas alone are the seed-principles of an ever-unfolding and transcendent revelation from the Creator to the creature.

The depth of significance in the one statement now before us that man is made in the image of God can never be exhausted. To develop the meaning of it, to discover this likeness in all its particulars, to realize the fact further and still further in new depths of our wonderful being, — this will be the history, I may say the only history of the spirit through eternity.

I believe this fact to be much more astonishing than is generally thought. Observe the high emphasis with which it is stated. "And God said, Let us make man in our image, and in our likeness, and let him have dominion. So God created man in his own image, in the image of God created he him." After finishing the wonderful work of creation, the whole of which may itself be said to be a stupendous image of the unseen spirit, in infinite shadow, cast from his being; after bringing out the endless hosts of the heavens and earth, an infinitude, an abyss of wisdom, — after this the Great Creating Power pauses, and designs a new and extraordinary creation, and as if nothing had yet been done in all the splendors of the fresh universe which shone and flamed with God, as if nothing had been done to exhibit the pattern of the invisible spirit, " God said, Let us make man in our image, after our likeness." Amazing, inconceivable work! If all this is as if no image, what is that to be which is to come forth as indeed the image of God? It was to be — Man! "So God created man in his own image."

I do not know how it can be that the infinite Eternal One, whose peculiar name was "Je-ho-vah," the one that is the " I am," the Being, a name or a description which while it asserts all reality of him denies and shuts out all attempts at conception, simply responding to inquiry, "I am," — I know not, I say, how this awful unknown one whose secret can never be penetrated, whose nature could not be described or expressed, could set forth man as the likeness or description of himself. But it is so. He is represented as a new creation, not of or a part of the other creation, but made after it, and made for the express purpose of imaging God.

If this be so, our first natural thought is, that we must expect to find that God, in every respect of which we can think of him, has a wonderful reflection of himself in us, a wonderful reflection of every characteristic, — a reflection, to be sure, as of the sun and of the whole sky in a bit of broken glass or in a drop of water, still a reflection. And it is so.

What a glorious image of his eternity is there in the endless life of the human soul, — that immortality which shall be fresh when the newest star shall fade, and before whose unshaken existence this creation or a thousand such yet to come forth shall pass away as the morning mists from the summits of the hills! Do you think that a mean image of the eternity of God? It is the fashion of many minds, and perhaps the prevalent one now, from a false humility or a false philosophy, practically to make light of the image of God in man. But it is too grand and solemn a heritage to be slighted, and I am not willing to believe that he who with such form and deliberation has made man to be in his own image has failed, or has met with inconsiderable success.

Think of any, even of what theologians call the "incommunicable," attributes of God (for my part I think there is no one of the characteristics of his adorable nature more incommunicable than another: in a sense they are all communicable; in another sense, none of them are so, but only the images or analogies of them); but look, I say, to any, even of the highest attributes of the divine nature, — his omniscience, for example, — that he is the universal day to which the light of knowledge in the soul of any man is indeed but as a few rays from that day struggling through a crevice into the narrow and dark room of the human spirit. Here, to be sure, is not likeness but endless unlikeness, — man not in the image of God. This is, however, but one aspect of it. Consider what a sublime thing it is to have conscious intelligence at all. " Man is a reed, but he is a thinking reed," says Pascal. And that one difference places him out of brotherhood with the whole universe, and places it far below his feet, and it leaves him no place or kin in the creation unless in alliance with God and those like God. And when you think that this holy spirit is so bounded and shut within his little tabernacle of clay, cabined, confined, hemmed in, you may be even awed by the force and reach of his thought, and that from its prison it struggles out into such likeness to divine intelligence. Not born, it seems, for one planet or for one range, this light follows the shining footprints of the creating God wherever they appear, and has built up for himself that enormous and complicated mass of mental achievement which we call our civilization, but which deserves to be called man's creation, — the evidence not only of his perceiving, but of his forming power. What will not such a power achieve when eternity is given to it for its growing-time, infinity for its sphere, and freedom from this small organism of the body into a spiritual liberty shall be its condition and state! Who shall fix the bounds of the circle it will describe? Reflecting thus, we cannot hold in contempt the fact that in man is also an image, if only an image, of the divine omniscience itself.

Or take again the incomprehensible statement that God exists everywhere. Have these thoughts and sympathies of ours which already can realize and hold before our consciousness beings most numerous, places most remote, — this soul, whose duty and power it is to be in communion with all that is holy everywhere in heaven or on earth, in past ages or in the present or in the time to come, which lives in the communion of the saints, and is now already come to Mount Zion, — is there in this not at least a fine shadow of the paternal image, which in its all-spreading presence communes at once with all that it has made?

Or look again at the creating power; is there nothing in what man does even like to this, even like the actings of that Being who made from chaos this most beautiful, and I might call it harmonious arrangement of things? For what is this which we call civilization but man's creation, man's world built upon God's world, — whence is it but from man's creating ideas shaping out of a savage crowd a world of society and state, shaping a world of religion and thought and science out of himself and out of his earth, shaping a world of beautiful things and useful things out of the rude heap he finds, — in all these wondrous workings, to be sure divinely inspired or divinely directed, but yet always a "co-worker with God," and the result an actual globe apart, a world of its own peculiar nature, built from the thought of man as the worlds issued from the thought of God, and exhibiting in little a beautiful image of the great creating attributes? Some image, then, of the whole of God is to be found within us.

But it was in the sweetness and innocency of the moral being of man that was to be found the most beautiful reflection of the divine image. What was the precise moral state of the first human being it is difficult for us now to say. There ought to be no doubt, however, among intelligent minds that the first created man was a fresh soul, with all the weakness and temptableness of a human heart and human passions, but yet unsoiled, as yet a happy and pure spirit in a happy and pure body, breathing naturally a childlike gratitude to the Being who appeared in everything as good and parental, and whose benign image stood about him everywhere in this new world on which his eyes were opened. I say this is the most rational view of the state of the first man, apart from the wonderful account in the Book of Genesis. And how sweet a picture, let me say, is all that divine history of the first days of man as the son of God! It is quite suitable to our ideas as we find it written there, that at this period the invisible One should delight in some suitable shape to appear and talk with man as with his friend. For the first man, though an innocent and noble creature, was yet ignorant and weak; and it is not only most beautiful to the imagination, but seems a truthful picture of facts, that at the first coming of the sun, or in the cool of the day when the wonderful luminary was sinking, or in the midst of the silent midnight and under the shining of the moon or of the more solemn starlight, — that at these times, or when there appeared some new object of fear or wonder or delight in the new universe, it was natural and beautiful and true, I doubt not, that the all-gracious Parent in some celestial shape communed with the first man, who was yet a child with the thought of a child, and that "solemn troops and sweet societies" of higher creatures were glad to surround his steps and supply the first wants of a being who had come among them with all the interest and tenderness which an infant brings into a household.

But this innocent image of God was but for a moment; man by transgression fell, and his childhood was gone, the divine simplicity of his spirit broken and defaced. But does the great history of the image of God stop here, ending in sad reverse and ruin upon Adam and his seed?

No; the fall of man opens a new and grand epoch in the history of God's image in the human soul. The creation of this material frame was finished at the beginning, but the creation of the spiritual life of man is a progressive act; it began then, only to be continued and expanded in a grander style thereafter. The fall of man, the loss of the image of his first innocence, was the moral chaos out of which he calls forth a new heavens and earth.

Listen to this wonder. You must have been struck

with the sentence spoken by God after the fall of man: "Man is become as one of us, to know good and evil." An increase, then, in the image of God; an awful likeness to the divine nature begun even then when he lost his innocence. By sin he gained the (in itself) dreadful knowledge of good and evil, — in itself an unspeakable loss, an unspeakable fall; but made by the divine goodness the means, the foundation on which a new and incomparably loftier image of the divine holiness could be built in the human spirit. Even by the fall he is born still further into the image of God, that dark descent allowing the divine mercy to lay deeper foundations and broader for a new building of the divine image. While man lost that innocence which was a sweet reflection of the moral purity of the Godhead, he gained by the enlargement of his experience, and I might almost say an enlargement of his being, the means or condition of building up a new and higher species of holiness, a more perfect image still of the Divine Being. For he who has fallen into the mystery of evil, if he be made capable of rising up from it, knows infinitely better than the innocent being can know the glory of holiness, acquires in that returning process moral qualities of incomparably more energy. But above all by allowing an opportunity for the mercy of God to show itself, acting through the sacrifice of his own Son, the fallen soul is penetrated with a depth of experience of what moral perfection is, as he sees it showing itself first in the form of an unspeakable justice, and then in the form of a far more unspeakable mercy; and so beholding this transcendent image "he is changed." A soul thus renewed is as much above the image of Adam, as Adam's innocence was above evil. Not a restoration, but an advance.

Thus wonderfully God wrought good out of evil, and made that which was purely evil but a stage in the process of developing his moral image in the soul of man. This new image of God is not like the childlike goodness, of ignorance of evil, which is but a distant resemblance to God's separation from evil. It has become a separation from evil such as God's is in the knowledge of evil; and, on the other hand, it has become an incomparable increase in the knowledge or appreciation of holiness, because holiness is a light which now shineth out of darkness and in contrast to darkness.

The innocent creature can know but little of God (whether it be man or angel); for what is God? Holiness, Justice, Mercy. And who knows the light of holiness that sees not the darkness of sin? Who knows justice that knows not wrong, and who knows mercy that knows not its forgiveness? The innocent creature, be it man or angel, can know little of himself, of his own nothingness and unworthiness, and he who knows not these things may speak of God, but knows him not as the utter rest and all in all of our spirits.

How vain these words are to tell of the wonderful image of God formed out of our ruin! To know the completeness of likeness which man may thus have to God, I point to the fact that the Being who is said to be himself the express image of the invisible, and the very brightness of his glory, he who was in the beginning with God, and was manifest in the flesh as man, — that this image is his; that he is the mould and model of it, and that the Christian soul is made a brother in his perfection and a sharer of every lineament of his image. There is something in this more wonderful than it has yet entered into our hearts to conceive.

And now we have seen that God in the beginning created man in his image, wonderful in all material respects and moral, and we have seen that he not only then created, but still creates; that through the deepest fall he makes new eras of enlarged perfection in this divine image. And what now shall be the future? With such a likeness to himself, thus amazingly created, through such sin, such agony of wretchedness, and the death of the first-begotten of God, I know not what future may be intended for man. The thing is unspeakable. We know not what we shall be, but this we know, that when he appears, the express image of God, we shall be like him; and in knowing that I think we know something which the tongue of no angel can utter.

Therefore, great and precious and albeit incredible

promises are left to men. They are to be kings and priests unto God. They are to judge the nations; they are to judge angels; they are to sit with Christ on thrones. "I appoint unto you kingdoms, even as my Father hath appointed unto me."

I do not so conceive of these promises as if these were to be dignities arbitrarily thrust upon man. Knowing that now the identical spirit which is one with Christ is one also with his people, I must look for this astonishing destiny of man; for this, if we saw it aright, is but the result of his astonishing character, which is oneness in the style, oneness in the image, of the divine Son of God.

If then any one be disposed to think meanly of this weak creature of the dust, to smile at his high pretensions, to make light of everything else, such as his knowledge or power, which can connect in likeness the unknown God with this worm, I will waive it all; but there is one thing I cannot waive. I cannot forget that the *logos* of God has been a man, that in the image of man he sits upon the throne, that he has made man his brother in moral glory now and in all dignity hereafter. I cannot deny this; nor do I wish to conceal or belittle it. I believe that the history of the world even so far (and things have but begun) has shown a fathomless meaning in the words which describe the creation of the first human being. "And God said, Let us make man in our image, after our likeness. So God created man in his own image, in the image of God created he him." I believe these wonderful words mark not a fact which was finished in Adam, but a fact which is ever finishing, the story of whose progress is the philosophy of the whole of history.

Let no one by a false humility put aside these things. God means that we should think greatly and yet more greatly of what he designs for the man who is his child. Judged by our *desert*, indeed, we should not be worthy to breathe even as worms of the dust; I believe earnestly that we are not entitled as a matter of right to a single sight of these heavens, to a single enjoyment or dignity even of this earth, but all the contrary. It is not possible for me to abase myself too low before my Judge, my Benefactor, my Saviour, my God! When I think one moment of God, of that greatness, of that purity, which makes the very heaven of heavens unclean; when I think of man, — "man born like the wild ass's colt," man "who drinks up his iniquity as water," it seems monstrous, blasphemous even to speak of him as in the image of God. It is the same feeling that ancient inspired singer felt when at night under a bright Eastern sky he sat contemplating the grandeur of the heavens, and of the God who formed them, and said, "When I consider thy heavens, the work of thy fingers; the moon and the stars, which thou hast ordained; what is man, that thou art mindful of him? and the son of man, that thou visitest him? For thou hast made him a little lower than the angels, and hast crowned him with glory and honor." The feeling here is precisely the feeling which becomes us. Our deserts we cannot regard too low: what is man? But the fact of the munificent gift and mercies of God to us, to be revealed in our souls and our destinies, we cannot exalt too high or enlarge too wide!

Let us then be of good cheer and great hope; for when God left the world, he left his image in man, as the image of the sun in drops of dew, or as the shadows on the earth when the sun has sunk. Every day and hour the enticements and low rewards of sin creep towards our hearts. When discouraged and in sorrow, let us remember the words, "God created man in his own image."

XVIII.

THE DECEPTION OF SIN.

Now the serpent was more subtile than any beast of the field which the Lord God had made: and he said unto the woman, Yea, hath God said, Ye shall not eat of every tree of the garden, etc. — GEN. iii. 1-24.

WHATEVER difficulties there may be, and are, if the early part of Genesis be viewed as literal history, or viewed as the imaginary embodiment of primitive and inspired conceptions, it is the most interesting record in the world. Nothing can be more weak and unhistorical than to read these narratives as if they were papers presented to a scientific convention, or as reports of a statistical bureau, or even that which we call biography or history. How literal they are no man will ever be able to say; but that they are truthful, in the deepest sense truthful, that they are a record of the very Spirit of God, no man competent to judge ought ever to doubt. Never was there such childlikeness in the form and the details, suiting the time, united with such dignity and depth of substance. Here is a tradition of the purest and profoundest ideas, issuing from the crude beginnings of the world; and here in pictured form are laid those great foundations of truth on which the human race is built, and without which it never could be truly human.

The Book of Genesis begins with God in action, with the creation of the heavens and the earth; and if it had stopped with the first sentence, " In the beginning God created the heaven and the earth," — that fact settled, everything is settled (I had almost said), for in that fact is laid the chief corner-stone of all truth; there is the fountain from which everything else flows. It means that spirit comes not from matter, but matter from spirit, and from such a spirit, an Almighty, which merely wills, and all that is stands up and says, "Behold us here!" — and that this one revelation not only stands first in order, but is so great that all subsequent revelations might be deduced or evolved from it; for if there is really an almighty spirit it must be all-pure also. And when I read that sentence, knowing that *that* is just the truth with which or without which everything must stand or fall, the sentence indeed and test, not merely of a standing or falling church, but of a standing or falling humanity, — I say no one can read it and look around to-day at the spirit of the latest sciences and philosophy, as they confront it, without a sense of heartfelt awe! After thousands of years the cleverest of the mere thought of the race writes its sentence: " In the beginning was the mere possibility of matter." Read that and this: " In the beginning God created the heaven and the earth."

The first two chapters, then, present and picture God

as Creator, creating the heaven and the earth. But leaving this, I come to the third chapter, which is my proper subject,— the beginning of the story of God in relation to his human child. Here begins the first incident of that story,— the fall of man. After just a glance at man innocent, we see man fallen.

The narrative is a very singular one, and for many years has been subject to much derision. A talking serpent, an apple, a deluded woman! For a long time this was taken to mean just what its outside looked. The Church has felt so superstitiously as to the Bible that it demanded all to be taken as bald and literal prose. But common-sense and the common taste of mankind show keen reaction from this, as all extremes make extremes,— swing from east to west, from utter credulity to scepticism. After a while, however, a higher order of interpretation arose; men were trained to value the significant traditions and legends of primitive times, and to treat them with reverence. Such critics see here a beautiful traditional poem as the form in which great truths are presented,— the historical symbol of our first parents in the garden, the fall and the expulsion, setting forth the inner history of our spirits as to good and evil,— a history not only true, but the most true; true of them and of each child of theirs.

Now, an interpreter of this class, while seeing here noble truths, might go further, and see also primitive and local colorings. I mean that he might see in the history signs of the human feelings and opinions of that far-off time and place. He might say, for example, I see here traces of the ancient Eastern feelings as to the character of woman. Adam in the account is comparatively innocent, or possibly high and generous, as the East would naturally think, and as our English poet thought, who says that he, seeing she had fallen, resolved through the vehemence of his love to perish with her, —

"from thy state
Mine never shall be parted, bliss or woe."

That is to say, this was a fall of woman, and rather an exaltation than a fall of man. In this way perhaps the narrative reflected the feeling of the time as to the superiority of man.

Then again, as the placing of Eve first and foremost in the weakness and transgression looks like a reflection from early human prejudices, so also the pre-eminent penalty upon the woman looks as if it sprang from that old Hebrew, and indeed human feeling, which, wherever it finds pre-eminent suffering, feels that it must be accounted for by pre-eminent guilt. The old world saw, as we see, that woman is the great sufferer of creation, so it thought that she must also be the great sinner.

And again; such a critic might go on to say, I see here the most ancient theory, or rather the most ancient imagination, now extant, of the origin of evil; namely, an evident tracing of it up gradually from the lower to the higher, from matter at the bottom through the serpent, through the weaker creature woman, up to man at the top. Its mysterious entrance is thus graded by minute steps, and is thus made more imaginable to us.

In such interpretations as these we get some idea of the tendency of modern criticism as to this narrative. But the Church at large does not consciously go so far. It goes very far to-day, in the fact which it more and more admits, that the form in which the creation and fall are described is a form divinely adapted and accommodated to man, and especially to the early ages of the world. Few thoughtful people will now venture to deny this; yet the intelligent application of it will resolve many of the difficulties.

As to the substance of the story of the fall, all believers concur that it is beautiful and divine. But what is its substance? It means that we are placed here on this earth, from the first man down, with a nature which may listen and ascend, or may listen and descend, capable of standing or falling. It means that the first parent heard a voice, and that we all hear a voice which says, "But of the fruit of the tree which is in the midst of the garden, ye shall not eat of it, neither shall ye touch it." It means that the warning carries with it solemn forebodings, — who has not heard them? "For in the day that thou eatest thereof thou shalt surely die." It means also that there is another voice which assures us and deceives us, — "Ye shall not surely die." So the fruit seems pleasant to the eyes, and glows rich through the foliage. We take; we eat. Thus seduced, the first parent ate and died, and we eat and die. As the first man did, so do we; and more than he, for in some measure we inherit a vicious will, which is entailed upon us. Who can deny all this? Not any one. And is not this original sin, derived sin? And is it not as certain as that the race-traits of the ancestors come down to the children?

Then, as to the form of the story: if any man does not like it, he must be, it seems to me, strongly wanting in the sense of the beautiful and the significant. Listen: "Now the serpent was more subtile than any beast of the field which the Lord God had made: and he said unto the woman, Yea, hath God said, Ye shall not eat of every tree of the garden? And the woman said unto the serpent, We may eat of the fruit of the trees of the garden: but of the fruit of the tree which is in the midst of the garden, God hath said, Ye shall not eat of it, neither shall ye touch it, lest ye die. And the serpent said unto the woman, Ye shall not surely die: for God doth know, that in the day ye eat thereof, then your eyes shall be opened; and ye shall be as gods, knowing good and evil."

What children we are to be quarrelling over a story of such deep import as that! What care I about the garden, this fruit, this talking serpent and his enticements? I know, alas! that a garden was, and the fruit, and the serpent, and that my first parent eating died, and that because of him and his weakness and sin I eat more readily and die more fully: there is the whole.

I will select two or three of the points of this narrative which most strike me. First, the truth of the serpent and his lie, — the truth, "Ye shall not surely die." It was true, the serpent had his truth. Strange to say, they did not die, as might have been expected, at once, by the fall of the great axe of justice. They lived on, and in their natural life felt perhaps little change, at least at the time. Again, he said, "Ye shall be as gods." True also; and the Lord God acknowledged the truth of the serpent's prediction when he said, "Behold, the man is become as one of us." But see the lie in both cases: first, as to death. Death did not come suddenly, as the crack of a rifle, or entirely; but, shooting and sprouting from that moment, gradually and really it did come, and always comes, entering first the heart of guilt, and creating immortal death there, and then by broken laws often or usually ruining the health and life of the body. And so by sin came death all through; we see then the serpent's lie.

Then as to the other point; namely, of man's becoming a god through sin and the opening of his eyes. Alas! their eyes were opened; they were as gods in knowledge. They, as it were, doubled their souls; the range of evil was added to the range of good: they became as gods. The old theology, which pictured primitive man not only as innocent but as superior, was not just. Sinful man is a larger creature than innocent man ever could be. Do you think an innocent earth-creature like that could ever have such a history of intelligence and power as ours, which is the history of a demon-man? Man did become as a god. But now see the lie. The gods standing in good see the evil as outside of them and against Him; but man, as one of the infernal gods, has gone down in evil, and standing in evil sees good there and evil here, — standing in conscious wrong sees his lost rectitude. The gods know good and evil, but not in the heart; man knows good and evil by partaking of evil, by sharing in it; and so in proportion to the elevation of his knowledge is the debasement of his soul. Man goes upward in a certain knowledge; but, passing in some sense upwards in light towards God, in a real sense he passes downwards in his being towards the Devil. That was the godlike advancement, — to have an illumined head but a darkened heart. So sin, the serpent, always palters with us " in a double sense." He promises the godlike and heavenly, but after all it is the way down to the bestial and demoniac.

See, then, what depth of meaning there is in all temptation! There is truth in it, to be sure, but a deeper lie is in it. There is some reality in the most empty things, a seducing charm in all evil, but just enough to lead us and land us in bitter wrong. Ah! here is the deception, the beautiful and deadly delusion, which lies in the path of all mortals, — wrong, fair at the entrance, but death at the end. No godhead awaits us in that path.

We have seen that there is a spirit which seems true

but is deeply false. See now the seeming falsehood but real truth of God. Adam did not die, and he was no doubt astonished. "In the day that thou eatest thereof thou shalt surely die." Untrue! They did not die. But yet God was true, most true in substance. Death, a deeper death in fact than they could anticipate, did follow their transgression, — always does; and though it was not a sudden and total extinction of being, as they may have imagined, yet even that imagination, though wrong in form, gave them in fact the most truthful glimpse they could have as to it. So not only was the substance most true, but the form, though in a sense false, was true in a far deeper sense; namely, in giving them an impression the most adequate possible, and the most correspondent to the fact.

In the beginning of this great record God gives us, if I may say so, this very principle of interpretation, the secret for which we are grasping every day. That is to say, we must always look in the Bible for a truth of substance; but as to the way it is presented, the form may sometimes be such as sacrifices the literal reality to the necessity of giving a truthful impression. If we tell a story to a child, we accommodate it to his mind, giving to his ignorance the most truthful impression it can receive.

Revelation was, as it is always, a dawning day which shows us a part of the landscape while the rest is in shadow. The eye of man is a darkened glass, and it cannot be cleared unless gradually and by experience.

If we look at this third chapter of Genesis, and at all this record of the beginning, what do we see but real and most vital truths, nobly expressed, but expressed to a child? It is so all through the Bible. When God at this enlightened moment says to the world, "God," "Redemption," "Immortality," we know his meaning, and yet we do not know it. At every stage of discovery, here and hereafter, God, redemption, and immortality will change to the eye, — though always the same, yet always widely different! Just as when he said "death" to the new-created woman Eve, she knew it and she knew it not. If a little boy — and every little child is like Adam, the man-child of the world — could recollect the lessons of his elders and gather them in a little book called his Genesis, his book of origins or beginnings, he would see the wisdom of his elders, not merely in the substance of the lessons, but even in their form; he would see just what we may see in this early Bible, which is God's primer for the childhood of the human race, on whose simple pages, though there are many things to which an archangel might listen with awe, they are often told with what I may venture to call beautiful child-talk.

The story of the fall suggests another thought. We are saved or we perish by one thing, — this: Have we or have we not trust in God? The Lord God told the woman one thing: "The fruit is deadly;" and the serpent told her another: "The fruit gives life." The veil was down, she could not see a step forward;

but the good voice, which she knew was good, told her that death was behind, and for a time she trusted that voice. But another voice, which was pleasant and seemed also reasonable, said pleasure and life were behind that veil; and though this persuasion went against what she knew to be good, she followed it. Had she but trusted!

Trust in the good thing. What is called faith is almost the one thought of the Bible. I might describe the whole of the Bible as the history of faith and of faithlessness, and here on the first page it begins. She, the trusting woman, — whose nature is trust, but who, alas! can often trust as easily in what seems good as in what is good, — she begins the world's woes, and begins them how? Through her perverted trustingness. The one secret of keeping and saving Paradise was, that man should rest entirely on what he knew to be good, should hold to that in the face of seduction. And just that also is the secret of regaining Paradise. If I have yielded to other voices, to hear again, though far off, the voice of the Son of God, to trust it, and in delightful, utter, childlike confidence to go back towards Paradise, that is all.

Know then that our first fall, and all our falls, are in false faith; that is to say, in trust in the Devil, trust in seeming good, and in want of an honorable, affectionate confidence in God and obedience to his sweet commands. Just here, we see, is all descent or ascent, fall or redemption!

Come, then, let us begin the right trust! Mercy can never be trusted enough. Our redemption always comes through faith, through the faith which reflects and says, "Yes, I am well aware that I have descended, — call it a fall. I am weak in will, selfish and low in affections; I yield to 'what is pleasant to the eye and seems good for food;' and I find that I have become a weak, poor soul, blurred and stained. But I know that the Redeemer liveth, and I will draw near again, for I know what is in his heart; and though I sin and fall from hour to hour, I will, whenever I recollect myself, be sorry for my sin, and say, 'I will trust thy forgiveness; I will trust thee forevermore.'" This is redemption, the recovery from the fall; this is divine ascent, — finding once more the regained Paradise in place of the Paradise which is lost!

XIX.

THE OBEDIENT SON.

Now his elder son was in the field: and as he came and drew nigh to the house, he heard music and dancing. And he called one of the servants, and asked what these things meant. And he said unto him, Thy brother is come; and thy father hath killed the fatted calf, because he hath received him safe and sound. And he was angry, and would not go in: therefore came his father out, and entreated him. And he, answering, said to his father, Lo, these many years do I serve thee, neither transgressed I at any time thy commandment; and yet thou never gavest me a kid, that I might make merry with my friends: But as soon as this thy son was come, which hath devoured thy living with harlots, thou hast killed for him the fatted calf. And he said unto him, Son, thou art ever with me; and all that I have is thine. It was meet that we should make merry, and be glad: for this thy brother was dead, and is alive again; and was lost, and is found. — LUKE xv. 25-32.

NO charge against Christ was more in vogue than that he thought too much of common and guilty people. In the fifteenth chapter of Luke's Gospel we find his defence of himself in respect to his tenderness to the lost, his habit of "receiving sinners." He answers, in effect, "My feeling is that of the true human heart, and of my Father's heart also;" and he tells several tales illustrating this,— of the man who lost one sheep in the wilderness; of the woman who lost one piece of silver; and, above all, that tale which is called the Parable of the Prodigal Son. So he defends himself.

He evidently thought that not merely Pharisees but even good people might feel justly hurt at the seeming preference for sinners; and so, to give full voice to this feeling, and then to answer the charge fully, he introduced the character of the obedient son, with his complaint and the reply to it. This obedient son seems at first an uninteresting part of the parable. It seems that he was in the field, and as he "drew nigh to the house, he heard music and dancing." It was not altogether unnatural that when he learned how his graceless brother had returned, and that for him was killed the fatted calf, he should at the first moment be angry; for he knew that in his way he had been true all his life, and none of this joy had ever been shown for him. So he refused to go in.

Note, first, the faults of this faithful son. He had been loyal, and was now jealous and angry, and more, he was proud and sulky; "he would not go in." Then "came his father out, and entreated him." But he is still indignant and resentful, and not at all backward to state and perhaps to overstate his own claims: "Lo, these many years do I serve thee, neither transgressed I at any time thy commandment." Nay, worse than all, he is not backward to make a complaint which is as cutting as it is bitter: "Yet thou never gavest me a kid [not to speak of a "fatted calf"], that I might make merry with my friends: but as soon as this thy son was come [mark the sneer], which hath devoured thy living with harlots, thou hast killed for him the fatted calf."

This son and his conduct suggest many thoughts to the mind. A chapter might easily be written on the faults of good men and the virtues of bad men, on the surprises of a good character and of a bad one. The faults of the good have a special ugliness because so unexpected and out of place, while the freshness and surprise of some instances of nobleness in a bad man come on us like the racy taste of wild fruit. I often think that taken together many saints and sinners are not so very far apart as they seem. We should not count that other men are all vicious because we do not like their style of sinning; nor, on the other hand, should we count that we have all virtue because we are respectable in some favorite points.

Let us consider especially the faults of dutiful people. Men who in the main are right seem on the strength of that to allow themselves in some sorts of fault. There are a thousand instances of this. An irritable man, for example, who feels, and justly, how much should be allowed to a nervous temperament, who knows that his tendency is often worse thought of than it deserves to be, and who confides in his general well-meaning, comes at length to indulge in habits of irritation and to have little or no conscience upon the point. A clergyman, who may be really a devout man, so assures himself on the good that is in him, and sometimes on his mere reputation for goodness, as to allow in himself quite a low tone of honor and a certain professional meanness; for all professions and all trades, I am sorry to say, have each their peculiar style of meanness. Again: there are good men in business and in public life who soon learn that in human affairs a certain freedom — shall I say a degree of unscrupulousness? — is most useful; so these men, though in the main they are just, and often on this very account, soon come unconsciously to a measure of freedom which may be called looseness. I know there is a false and feeble scrupulosity which unfits for life, and which the very best men are rarely subject to; but I am afraid this is a truth scarcely safe to trust in the hands of the world at large. He is a rare statesman, and he is a rare man of business, who without a trace of weak scrupulosity is always truly honorable. Again: a regular and obedient Christian may insensibly take on a certain pride and a certain claim in religion, so that when, for example, he hears the parable about paying the full penny to him who comes in at the eleventh hour, and no more to him who has "borne the burden and heat of the day," he feels a sense of injustice. And this is the case as to the tale before us; for while to the mass of men it is the most beautiful word ever uttered, I have no doubt that to some very regular and excellent people the part as to the prodigal is not free from distastefulness. They feel as this elder brother felt. The injustice done to himself, to his excellent and hard-worked self, quite swallows up his natural joy over his recovered brother, quite treads out his humanity.

Observe in two or three cases how this self-complacent feeling acts. Regular people, for example, tend to certain extreme prejudices, especially prejudices against particular classes of irregular people, — " sinners." We have our pet aversions in the moral world. The honorable merchant, who does not steal, feels that theft breaks all the code. The respectable woman is cruel to her outcast sister, and she will not be melted even if the prodigal is penitent. The man who by long years has grown steady in good habits looks with more than suspicion upon sudden changes called " conversions." The change of the thief on the cross is not a natural thing to him, and is only believed because it is in the Bible. And so on.

Now this style of good men need a reprimand; they are not so good as they seem. Indeed, I must say that as the two figures stand here together, one's sympathies may best go with the young prodigal.

In the second place, observe the father's treatment of this dutiful son. The son " was angry and would not go in: therefore came his father out and entreated him " to go in, and gave him two reasons. The first is this: " Son, thou art ever with me, and all that I have is thine," — that is, I have done no injustice; I am fair to you. This especial overflow of kindness to the prodigal is an occasion, but I am ever with thee; this music and the fatted calf are a momentary gift, but all that I have is thine. You have not asked your portion of goods and squandered it; it is all thine. I welcome, to be sure, my lost son, and it is true that during this moment of joy I value more the lost piece of silver, the lost child, than that which is always with me, — that is human, — and it is true that so far as may be I will reinstate him; but still the lost heritage returns not: what is lost is lost. Yours is the unlost heritage.

Now, in this part of the parable, we see, is the necessary correction to the lavish kindness, the abandonment, of the prodigal's reception. Far be it from me to neutralize the beautiful welcome the Father of prodigals bestows upon his returning children. That "welcome home again" to every soul which cries out, "I will arise," has gone down into the very heart of the world. Every ear hears it, and it lifts, if only for a moment, every drooping head. No deeper revelation has ever been made of the heart of God. That divine Son who has taught us all to say, "Our Father," has here raised still higher the curtain which covers the pathos of the Father's heart. Still, we must not be one-sided. Even the Father's pity cannot do everything. Sin, wrong, even redeemed and forgiven wrong, has a solemn aspect. Broken laws will have at least something of their vengeance. We see it in nature. A foolish course is changed, the bad man grows better, a new robe is on him, but something of violated law still follows him, and broken health, and lost honor, and wasted fortune will not come back at command. And though the God and

Saviour in the Gospel is far above nature, far kinder than the God in nature, yet even in that kingdom of kindness — "kingdom of grace," as we beautifully call it — we see that the man who has abused his soul will thereby suffer loss, even after he has come home. The portion that fell to him is gone, and though he may recover much, there are things he cannot recover. Nothing can make up for the evil of bad habits. To be sure, a great awakening at the centre, a glowing fire in the heart, may break through the crust of deadly habit for a time; but there is fear that, unless that fire burns intensely or very long, old things will resume their place. You may return to the Father's house with the sound of music, but when you are back there and settled, a life of struggle may be before you. You carry back into the temple a desecrated soul, and it must be built again from its own ruins. The region of religion, though it is above nature in that it admits of greater redeeming changes, is, after all, a region of law. It is true that, if the prodigal's gratitude and love are as great as the sins from which he is saved, there may be a good in the calling forth of these qualities which will be more than a compensation for the evil; and I believe that there are renewed souls which reascend higher by far than the more regular and obedient children; but as a rule, a permanent obedience, good habits, an unperverted imagination, a will for good long strengthened, an unsquandered soul, are better than the fatted calf and the music, however heavenly, of the great sinner pardoned.

We may reach a higher good by the knowledge of evil, if the Spirit given to us is full enough. There is always hope for the most inveterately wicked. But this is not the rule; for a prodigality and an inveteracy of evil usually break the very springs of good in the soul, and though such a man may repent and trust and be forgiven, his nature, so far as we can observe it, rarely quite recovers, and it would seem that his destiny hereafter will be on a lower level than it might have been.

The lot of the obedient son is one deeply enviable, and God is not unjust. If, then, you have tried to do your duty, and repine over the fact that your life is uncheered by music within or without, if your heart is slow and dull, your outward fortunes poor, while you see fortune's favors around you in the world, and, what is worse, even in the kingdom of God, — that is, see sinful men and women coming from afar and reaching as if in a moment what you have been toiling all your life to find, and if you hear the angels of God rejoicing over them and not over you, still, be steady. "Son, thou art ever with me, and all that I have is thine."

This, then, is the father's first argument with his obedient but complaining son. His next and finer appeal is addressed to the better heart of this son. Listen: "Son, it was meet that we should make merry and be glad: for this thy brother was dead, and is alive again; and was lost, and is found." Observe: "It was meet that *we*" — you as well as I — "should make merry: for this *thy brother*" — not this my son only — "was dead, and is alive again." This simple appeal, — not to justice only, or to the generous and tender heart, but this call to *family* mercy, — this entreaty to human brothers that they should feel he same domestic love the Father feels, — this is a revelation to us all of the heart of the Father of the house. "It was meet." If there hears me any father or any mother, any parent who has known that heart-break, a lost son, who has seen him squalid and broken, but returning, and who knows what a thrill of tender joy would welcome the lost boy, stained and wasted, but with the tears of penitence upon his cheek, coming back and saying, "Father, mother, I have sinned," that parent's heart will know the deep truth of the appeal, "It was meet." The regular son, the cold man of duty, needed to be converted to something higher, — to love; and so the father says to him, "It is meet." He is treated with charming wisdom and pathetic sweetness, — no less, I think, than is the prodigal.

The story is usually called the Parable of the Prodigal Son; but it seems to me more properly a tale of the fatherhood of God, or, if it must be named anything else, it should be a tale of the father and his two sons. The whole world, conscious of sin, has risen up in response to that one vision, — of God seeing afar off his lost son; but has it seen as clearly the exquisitely balanced feeling of the tale, — the father turning now to one child, and now to the other, turning from gross sin to the pride of duty, and entreating that also to return and to be humble, merciful, brotherly? If we are charmed that God is such a Father to us as prodigals, we may be charmed also that he is so forbearing to us as conceited and intolerant men of duty. Ah! we must guard against the vices even of our virtues. Good conduct is always near to pride, and pride is near to great expectations and claims, and these disappointed are near to bitterness towards God and envy of others: "I deserved something, and have not got it; he deserved nothing, and see how he prospers."

God seems to me more endearing when he forbears towards pride, and entreats it, than when he forgives open sin. He would have been just had he said, "You, with all your duty, are yet a conceited, selfish, and hard-hearted creature; you do not serve God for naught,—not you; you have no feeling for your destroyed brother; you are thinking how much he gets and how little you get; you want a kid; you forget the nobleness of your privileges,—'Son, thou art ever with me, and all that I have is thine;' you forget the inherent good of the faithful sons of God,—that the Lord is your portion, the lot of your inheritance; and you are angry. Go, ingrate, and learn that lowliness is better than proud duty, that mercy to the prodigal is better than to keep all the commandments. Go!" That would have been just; but that was not the heart of the father. He entreats him to go in, and says: "Son, thou art ever with me, and all that I have is thine. It was meet that we should make merry and be glad: for this thy brother was dead, and is alive again; and was lost, and is found."

O beautiful vision of God! most precious to the sinful sons of men! On that hand, for foolish prodigals perishing with hunger, he has "bread enough;" and on this hand, if we have tried to do some duty, to toil along in the life of hard work, but are yet, though dutiful, cold hearts, a sort of miserable officials and complainers, he yet bears it, and is more than just to us, and entreats us. This poor race of ours has to thank its Lord and Saviour for many things; but is there anything really so precious to us as this, — to know that whether we be prodigals or sinful men of duty, whatever we are, we have such a God as this, a Father who knows all our weaknesses and remembers that the best of us are but dust, — that "this God is our God for ever and ever"?

XX.

CHRIST AND THE GADARENES.

Then the whole multitude of the country of the Gadarenes round about besought him to depart from them; for they were taken with great fear. And he went up into the ship, and returned back again. Now, the man out of whom the devils were departed, besought him that he might be with him: but Jesus sent him away, saying, Return to thine own house, and show how great things God hath done unto thee. — LUKE viii. 37-39.

CHRIST had cast out the devils from this man, and had destroyed a herd of swine. Then the people "besought him to depart from them; for they were taken with great fear." Here is almost the only instance in the New Testament where Christ appears with something of terribleness in his power, so that to the frightened imagination he seemed a vaguely terrible being, and they besought him to depart.

Fear as to the supernatural, particularly if it spreads through a multitude, as it did here, is the wildest of the passions, and quite overthrows our weak souls. For we *are* weak, ignorant, and sinful creatures, and precisely because of each of these, — weakness, ignorance, sinfulness, — we fear. Nay, if even God would afford to our reason every pledge of safety, we should still instinctively tremble before unknown power. The Israelites were profoundly alarmed before Sinai; and the apostles could not behold some of the miracles of the gentle and beloved Master without the deepest agitation. But here was an act, not only of terrible, but of destroying power; and so " they were taken with great fear."

This singular exception in the career of Christ forcibly impresses us with the fact of his usual gentleness, of his general care not to alarm a creature so easily alarmed. This is well worthy of attention. As it is almost impossible to wield supernatural power without exciting alarm, we can see how wonderfully in his hands its terrors were subdued. Take up these Gospel narratives, and we find crowded into a period of from one year to three such an imposing mass of wonders, such displays of more than mortal power, that if they were fully believed in, as they were, they would startle the soul to its depths with terror. But they did not, because of the mild and sympathetic style of the miracles themselves; also, of the instinctive confidence of the heart, not only in Christ's thorough humanity, but in his humaneness; and because all this mighty force was clearly used, not for personal ends or from personal wishes, but by a being thoroughly righteous. More than this: had he been merely righteous, what to sinful men could have been more terrible than a being of supernatural energies walking among them with a heart of mere justice? From such a being the whole world would fall back.

There must, then, have been inspired, wherever he appeared, such a deep sense of benignity, such a feeling that all this strange power was in the hands of unselfishness and mercy, that so, and so alone, the frightfulness of mere might, or even of just might, was covered over and made tolerable and even sweet. It was true of him, as Job sublimely says of God, that he held "back the face of his throne."

The God in Nature, as we see him working around us, shows the same spirit which was in Christ. As his Father worked, so he worked. Through all these mighty operations in the universe, passing on even now, all is done with unspeakable quietness; the heavens are held up in silence, the great oceans and rivers are heard in whispers; the power is hushed, as a mother stills the noises which would alarm a sleeping child. If I were to express what is perhaps the most striking impression of this creation, I should call it gentleness, — a gentleness like that of Christ. Without this it is obvious man could not exist, much less enjoy, or be trained for his destiny. It is true this concealment of power seems to be carried far, so that man almost loses the sense of that awful Presence which is among us. Hence God startles us, exceptionally, with events which we call miracles. In these, the very person of God comes in, or stands at the door and knocks. Without something of this we should lose God in the hush of his gentleness, in the soundless harmony of perfect and unchanging law. But the regularity and gentleness are his custom;

and even when it is necessary that he should walk into the scene himself, though he comes with a startle, he comes with no terror, but appears under the sweet humanity and with the humane ways of Christ.

But the Gadarenes were afraid, not merely because of his supernatural terribleness, but because of a much more vulgar reason: they saw the loss of property, the drowning of the swine. "This stranger may bring very high things with him; indeed, that is clear, for he ejects devils;" this could not be denied. But these men were much more sensitive to their lower than to their higher interest. "Suppose he does come as a dispossessor of devils, — we don't wish our swine destroyed." Look at this fact of human nature: he came, as we know, bringing wherever he came the very kingdom of God; but then the swine were destroyed! So they "besought him to depart from them." They recognized the majesty of Christ, just as multitudes of us do to-day; but then it is disagreeable; it interferes with property, with pleasures; and they, as we, wish him away.

In this, the city and region of Gadara were an exact image of the whole Jewish nation. He came to the Jews at the last hour of their hopes, when the State and the people were sinking into a great gulf, and whether he was the Messiah of the prophets or not, no man can deny that he was the true and only Messiah for them, who, if he had been received, would have given them a divine revelation and purification and power, and established them forever on the tops of the mountains. But the men of Gadara were taken with a great fear, — their swine; the high Pharisees and rulers at Jerusalem were also taken with a great fear, — *their* swine: their places, power, prejudices, all threatened. As Gadara was, so was Jerusalem; and as Jerusalem was, so men are in all places and times.

True; and not merely of Christ, but of every one like him who brings to men something higher than they want, and menaces them with any mean loss. Let it be a patriot, a reformer, a truth-teller of any sort, he must depart.

All good comes into the unwilling heart as a disturber. Every gleam and monition and persuasion which says, " My son, this is the path of life," — all this, terrible or beautiful as the voice may be, is uncongenial. We are fond of such poor things that the pure and right thing is an interference. But God will interfere. He is the sternest of disturbers, for all his mercy prompts to our disturbance. He aims to shake us out of our delusions, though we cry, " Hold! " He stings and spurs; and the more he stings and spurs, the more he thinks of us; and only when he thinks not of us, — when we have become as brutes, — only then he gives us entire ease, and leaves our coasts.

Here, then, was one prayer and its answer. But we have another: " Now the man out of whom the devils were departed besought him that he might be with him." Ah, how different the petition! This was he who had lately said, " What have I to do with thee? I beseech thee, torment me not." But the devils were gone now, and he was clothed and in his right mind. He "besought him that he might be with him."

This stands here to every age a model and an image, as fine as any, of the spirit redeemed, — the power of Satan fallen off, — and the whole heart lifting itself to its gracious Deliverer. This man had passed from darkness to light; from the power of Satan unto God; from the cry, "What have I to do with thee, Jesus, thou Son of God most high?" to "Master, let me be with thee."

Here, then, were two prayers, — the one embracing, the other ejecting, the Lord of life; the mass on the one hand, and the rare exception on the other; the poor outcast here, the prosperous citizens of Gadara there.

Mark the contrast of these two prayers, also their answers. "They besought him to depart; and he went up into the ship, and returned back again," — a prayer granted. "Now the man out of whom the devils were departed besought him that he might be with him; but Jesus sent him away," — a prayer refused.

The one prayer granted. These "fat and greasy citizens," who wanted nothing but the world, had their way, just as they wished it. The Lord granted them their request, but sent leanness into their souls.

But consider the other prayer, — the prayer refused. Here was a poor creature, the man dispossessed, who had been all shaken with his spiritual and bodily pests, indeed quite shattered; and now that he felt the blessed peace and purity of health, and looked on the past

"Like a phantasma, or a hideous dream,"—

seeing, in fact, the terrible figures which had possessed him retreating but still menacing, he shrunk frightened to the feet of his Benefactor, and clung there like a child. He was afraid to be left alone; he was most grateful and tender towards the pitiful Being who had relieved him. "Master, I am grateful; let me attend thee and serve thee wherever thou goest; let thy home be my home. Master, I adore thee; let me be with thee. This night of the devil may return; with thee I am safe: let me go with thee. These who thus dismiss thee have not known thee; let me be with thee."

Could such a prayer be denied, and by the pitiful Lord? It was denied: "But Jesus sent him away." Scarcely anything in the story of Christ looks sterner. I believe it is the only final denial he ever gave to any affectionate petition for aid. I cannot recall that he ever refused before; and why here? We scarcely know why. It would have saved the poor creature from so much! But it was denied. We cannot explain the divine ways, whether in Nature, in history, or in the Gospels. They are often very far above, out of our sight. Do we not all know of deep wishes of the heart which, if they could have been granted, would have saved much, not merely of sorrow (for sorrow is a blessed thing), but of guilt? Alas! I cannot explain.

There is, I doubt not, a great end, where all the threads and lines are gathered and drawn in together in one result; and that, I hope, will explain all.

However, we can see something. Though God trains us, and not according to our methods, yet we can often see that he is the true Master of discipline. In this case it seemed pleasant and safe to be with Christ; but the man needed strengthening of the will, strong habits. God knows it is best that we should struggle through difficulty. Easiness is not for us. The Lord demanded a manhood of the soul. He said to his apostles, when leaving the world, "It is expedient for you that I go away;" and then, besides, he opened to this man the great resource of doing something: "Return to thine own house, and show how great things God hath done unto thee. Make good your standing-place here, in the spot where you are; here show forth your gratitude."

Observe in this the controlled feeling and wisdom of Christ. He yields to none of the weak wishes of love. "Find my presence and safeguard not in this place or that, but in duty, wherever that is; show your adoration and gratitude, and work out the sublime life you propose to yourself, not in the wish to follow me, but just here, in this spot, distant and obscure as it is, and in doing work like mine." So he commits the man to himself, as the bird commits its fledgling to the air, to use its own efforts for flight, and to beat with its own wings against the currents of the strongest winds.

Here, then, was a prayer, refused indeed, but granted while it was refused. The real under-wish of the heart, which was, to be kept safe in the true good, was granted — and best granted — by this refusal.

So in both these cases the real wishes were responded to: he gave both in reality what they sought. He gave the fat citizens the safe enjoyment of their swine; and while he told his poor friend that he must leave him, he yet gave himself back to him in a higher manner. And just this God always and accurately does. God is always the hearer of prayer. He hears the wicked as well as the righteous. He hears all prayer but sham prayer, and that is no prayer. Whatever the heart really wants, and persists in wanting, he grants. If we wish him away, we may be sure " he will go up into the ship, and return back again; " if we really wish to be with him, though he seems to depart, he never departs. Substantially, whatever we want, we shall have. There are but two lives, — the life of the earth and that of heaven. If our prayer is that heaven may disappear, and leave us to the earth, just as certainly as heaven departed from the men of Gadara it will depart from us. " He that seeketh findeth; and to him that knocketh it shall be opened." This is no magic, or exception, or favoritism: it is the law of the spiritual world, and is as certain as our existence.

Hear, then, again the text, and let its deep spiritual meaning be forever written upon our hearts: "Then the whole multitude of the country of the Gadarenes round about besought him to depart from them; for they were taken with great fear. And he went up into the ship, and returned back again. Now, the man out of whom the devils were departed, besought him that he might be with him: but Jesus sent him away, saying, Return to thine own house, and show how great things God hath done unto thee."

XXI.

MAN'S PRAISE MORE THAN GOD'S PRAISE.

For they loved the praise of men more than the praise of God. — JOHN xii. 43.

THE hunger of praise takes a thousand forms, and is often disguised; but I think it is the most universal and deepest passion of our hearts, certainly of many hearts, and there is no nature, however dull, which is not keenly alive to it. It breathes through all souls, from the little child up. Not the most distinguished actor on the most illustrious stage of the world, not the admired woman in the pride of her beauty, or the unadmired woman in the subdued yet eager aspirations of her heart, — not these are more marked by it than the begrimed sweep coming out of his home in the chimneys. The hod-carrier honestly prides himself on his quickness and strength, and he too is for having his admirers. We all, in different degrees, wait upon, hang upon, pant for good opinion. The affectionate heart longs for it in its highest shape of kindness and love; the vain long for their petty applause, and those who are too proud to own it, who pretend to rest on themselves, are often half-dying for praise; but then, it must be in some form choice enough and large enough to suit their pride. The clackings of a little town or a little newspaper satisfy some; the trumpet of the ages is the want of others.

To be sure, some of the higher order of men, in their love for pure truth or for humanity, outgrow much desire for mere praise. The true thinker loves his thought better than the pay or praise. When a traveller visited the study of the illustrious A. von Humboldt, he found all his splendid orders and insignia which were gifts from the most distinguished bodies and men in Europe, — he found them all thrown in a heap in the corner of the room. And yet even Humboldt would have been keenly sensitive to the loss of his true renown, and all alive to any real disgrace. Ineradicable is that feeling. In fact, few men ever realize how much it is to them. When deserted by some people we fall back upon the good opinion of some others, and never until we have that rare experience of being deserted by all, and not only neglected but hissed by all, — not until that does any man know the deep dependence of his heart upon the opinion of his fellows.

So deep a passion must have a great and benign purpose. The bad things in this creation of God always, if fairly looked at, betray a deep good below; and so it is here. Praise sets the whole world in motion to useful ends. There are moments when if we have it fully we feel as if borne upon the most beautiful and softest cloud of the sunset, and sunk to rest within its gorgeous down; but if we have it not, we are poor and naked. If the work of the world were actuated merely by the hunger and thirst of the senses, all work would stop except mere brutal clutchings, and man's life become as poor and cheap as the life of the beasts. On the other hand, were we actuated to work merely by duty, what slack workmen should we be! How still and nerveless the industry of the earth! And if we were left to the love of truth or beauty, — the truth-instinct and the art-instinct, — how faint and cold are they, except to a very few indeed! But when the warm master-passion comes in, then with infinite pains we dress the body to please the eye of man; we build and furnish fine houses for the eye of man; we surround ourselves with splendors of art to meet the eye of man; make science, philosophy, and literature for the applause of man. We are drudges for money to support it all, and so, moved by praise, we build up the world. It is a magical passion, in short, which works more wonders in an hour than all the magicians; but, like everything else within us, it has gone wrong. Man usurps the whole field of our vision, and God is left out. We love "the praise of men more than the praise of God."

There is no blame expressed for our loving the praise of men, but for loving it more than the praise of God. We were made to be alive to the approbation of man as well as of God, not of one but of both, — alive, however, to the lower while under and ruled by the higher. But our whole hearts have gone to man, and we "worship and serve the creature more than the Creator." It would not be so bad to sink down and be governed by man's opinion if we confined ourselves to the right sort of men. There is something very high in approving ourselves to the best society of the earth; but usually we care little for that. It is the poor opinion of some little set we care for; and the lower their aims and the lower their taste, so they be in vogue, the more naturally are they our gods; for the worshipper and the god must be somewhat on a level. We hear the slightest whisper of this low, petty opinion as if we had diseased ears; and we feel the poorest sneer or laugh as if we were cut by the sting of a whip. Oh, teach your child contempt for mean opinion! Give to his nature a manly hardihood to throw it off as water from a rock.

I read very early in my youth a novel of which I remember only the motto, but that is ineffaceable, — "They say. What say they? Let them say." Where the favor of man is made the object of the soul, ask three questions about it, — What is it? What can it do? How can it be got?

Is it pure, discerning, judicious opinion we are swayed by? Nay, it is impure, undiscerning, trifling. Or is it honest and heartfelt? Nay, it is shallow and from the lips. Or is it honorable, faithful, steady? Nay, "favor is deceitful." Alas! who has not felt its changes? I once had near my window a beautiful tree, which became at last like a living, conscious thing to me. I used to watch it in the summer. How graciously the soft airs caressed it and played with it! But in the winter the airs were turned into raging winds, which tore it and rent it. So the same kindly opinion which in the sweet summer comes as a breeze and whispers about us and moves the world of leaves with beauty and grace, — the same treacherous air soon comes as the winter's wind, seizes and strips the tree, buffets and harasses and strains it, through the dark days and stormy nights. Such are the changes of human favor.

> "Blow, blow, thou winter wind,
> Thou art not so unkind
> As man's ingratitude;
>
> . . . . . .
>
> Freeze, freeze, thou bitter sky,
> Thou dost not bite so nigh
> As benefits forgot."

And what can this favor do for us? Much, I grant; but can it do anything in great emergencies? If not, then at best it is not beyond a holiday good. And then, see how hard a thing it is to get. A mere chance controls it, for the judge who awards it is blind, or corrupt and won't see. Nay, and look at the expense of it, — the expense of sorrow and pain to others who are my rivals, I treading them down; and then the expensive waste in the prostitution of myself, for no man reaches this favor and keeps it, and keeps also himself unspoiled.

I might grant, then, that the favor of man is a sweet and good thing, but when it is made the first thing, I see unhappiness follow in every sphere; I see how this poor mistaken creature, aspiring and aspiring, only meets disappointments; I see how after a world of efforts and anxieties he is pitilessly forgotten or even sneered out of the world. And oh, think of the sin of it, of the vulgar pride and impudence of success, of the black discontent and malignity of failure!

The text was uttered about whom? About the highest men in Judea. "Nevertheless, among the chief rulers also many believed on him; but because of the Pharisees they did not confess him; . . . for they loved the praise of men more than the praise of God." They preferred that the highest Being their eyes had ever seen should go on unrecognized, persecuted, outcast, and exposed to death, because the fashion was against him, and they were afraid to risk anything of their precious position in the synagogue. Yes, and all our best native impulses are thus forced down because we also are afraid. Nay, we sink even below honor and common tone because we are afraid of man.

And who is this of whom we are afraid, — this creature ignorant in his eyes, and feeble or malignant in his heart? Who is he? What is he? "Afraid of a man that shall die, and of the son of man which shall be made as grass, and forget the Lord our Maker!" Oh, we foolish little people who can't be happy and can't even be manly until other foolish people allow us to be! Trimming our souls to suit others; harassing ourselves to the bone to meet somebody's approval; striving with our fellow in a sort of hostile scramble for the crumbs of the world's favor, or pining and bitter if it is lost!

He who waits on God is nothing of this style of person. Praise or blame falls off the surface of his soul whose whole being is a love and a fear of something infinitely lovelier than your praise and infinitely more fearful than your blame. He that waiteth on the Lord renews his strength. He likes kindly opinion, of course, especially of high-thinking people, but he can do without even that.

All the world thinks highly of George Washington to-day. His life is a good book to read, especially for Americans. I wish we would read it, and think as we read, for there is far more real religion in his life than in most religious books. The chief thing I find about him is that he had a higher instinct than for praise. At all times, but especially during the struggle of the war, he had hard things to bear. He was misunderstood, underrated by inferior men, conspired against, traduced; yet his course is marked throughout by a singular magnanimity towards enemies and towards lukewarm friends. Did he not feel? He deeply felt all the baseness, but he had a deeper feeling; namely, that he could step down and forfeit everything with equanimity because he sought something higher even than honorable fame, — the good of his country, obedience to duty, the will of God.

So it is with every Christian man. If there is a storm without, he knows a divine pavilion whereunto he may always resort. Paul said, "With me it is a very small thing that I should be judged of you, or of man's judgment." That seems like pride. No, it was pure height. It was the same spirit as his Master's. His Master loved true praise, — loved the recognition of right souls. Never was there a more spontaneous outburst of satisfaction than when he found that Simon Peter recognized him — recognized his value — who he was. "Thou art the Christ, the Son of the living God." "Blessed art thou, Simon Bar-jona: for flesh and blood hath not revealed it unto thee, but my Father which is in heaven." Yet he could do without recognition, and when there was not one voice to hail him, when the world was unanimous against him, in that solitude of the earth, "They have left me alone," he said, "yet I am not alone, because the Father is with me." When he heard nothing but one loud hiss from the earth, he said, "I do always those things that please him."

Who wants peace, then? Who wants dignity of life? Let him follow Christ, approve himself to God, and be at peace. He who does that has reached three things. He can do without man; that is something. Next, he can be firm and even content if you give him a bad name, — the hardest trial a sensitive spirit ever meets. Nay, beyond this he can say, — at least there was one who could, — "I can glory in shame."

Oh, if a man can ever live to say, "I care much for good opinion, but I care more to do right, and I care more still for the opinion of God; I live and labor through the hours of each day, not so much to be greater in any man's eyes, — to be a little richer, a little more distinguished, — but to be a little more just, more magnanimous, more generous, for God loves generosity, magnanimity, and justice; and if I strive to do those things he loves, he will be merciful to me in all my sins, even as I am merciful to others, and his divine redemption will cleanse me from all stains, — thus loving the praise of God more than the praise of men, thus studying to show myself approved unto God, thus seeking for true honor and immortality, the result will be that, whether living, dying, or dead, I shall have honor and immortality; that is, his gracious approval, his countenance which is life, his reconciled presence where there is fulness of joy and pleasures forevermore."

XXII.

THE GOOD SAMARITAN.

And behold, a certain lawyer stood up, and tempted him, saying, Master, what shall I do to inherit eternal life? etc. — LUKE x. 25-38.

"A CERTAIN lawyer stood up, and tempted him," — put him to the test. Why? Because the freedom and originality of Christ's words — breaking into sabbatical views, etc. — had made him the great heretic of the day to the orthodox Jew; so it is quite curious to see the numerous attempts made to test him. This testing was usually from malice, and a wish to destroy his authority, sometimes from curiosity and fondness for debate, and in the present case possibly from a real desire to learn.

"Master, what shall I do to inherit eternal life?" It seems an inquiry personal and serious. And the Master answered, "What is written in the law? how readest thou?" He referred him to Moses; for in the spirit of true progress he assumed as little as possible the position of an original authority, and always based the new gospel on a higher interpretation and development of the old truth. "And the lawyer, answering, said unto him, Thou shalt love the Lord thy God with all thy heart, and with all thy soul, and with all thy strength, and with all thy mind; and thy neighbor as thyself."

Now this masterly falling back from the tree to its root, from the whole world of Jewish law, which spread like the branchery of a huge tree, to its two great trunks or roots, and then the naming of these, not fear to God and justice to man, but love,—this magnificent reduction to great principles we often ascribe to Christ; but I think we err in doing so, for it is here found in the mouth of a Jew as a thing commonly understood, and it is clearly found in the books of Leviticus and Deuteronomy. Still, though it was known, practically it was not known. It was only grasped at by a few, and not practically realized even by them. But from the lips of Christ it took a new reality. As he spoke it, the moral law was not only brought to its deepest roots and made complete, but it was also made the law of the heart. Yet no; not quite complete. One great point was still left undetermined. Love to God, love to my neighbor, the substance of the law was. Yes; but who is my neighbor? In the old time under Moses it was, not man, but a brother-Hebrew. Nay, narrower than that, it was confined to Hebrews not unclean, not slaves, etc. Even when ages had gone by, and when prophets seemed to catch wider glimpses, broad lightning-flashes of duty, illuminating a broader neighborhood, a wider landscape of humanity, it was, like the lightning, only for a moment, and then the broad vision seemed to contract itself again into as narrow a neighborhood as at the first, so that at the time of Christ the wall of partition still rose around them like a citadel thronged with fiery shapes of hate, of prejudice, of war, against the whole earth.

The Jews, then, needed two things: First, towards God, they needed the word "love" in place of all other words; Secondly, they needed that the word "neighbor" should be interpreted by a wide heart. So the lawyer who asked "Who is my neighbor?" asked *the* question which the Hebrew race at that critical epoch was bound to answer; for the penalty of the human race was about to fall on the unneighborly, narrow Jew, as upon the hater of the human race. The Roman eagle, turned into the Roman vulture, was waiting for its victim. A question then indeed it was, "Master, who is my neighbor?" The answer is the parable of the Good Samaritan.

This answer is, in the manner of Christ, a little story, a brief word; and we will consider it. The answer might have been a dry definition; but, far from that, it came from Christ's heart in the shape of a story filled with imagination and feeling. "A certain man went down from Jerusalem to Jericho." Immediately the crowd around him are lost in eager interest. It is to be the story of a man travelling a fearful road, which descended from the heights of Jerusalem, and going down through gorges and abrupt defiles was the chosen haunt of wild robbers and was well known as a terror. "A certain man went down from Jerusalem to Jericho, and fell among thieves, which stripped him of his raiment, and wounded him, and departed, leaving him half dead." It is done; there he lies, wounded, frightened, helpless. But "by chance there came down a certain priest that way." There was a great station for priests down at Jericho, and one of their number was now travelling up to his duties in the temple. The poor wounded creature, at the side of the road, lying and listening, hears the coming of some one. It is a priest, the first sight of whom seems life; but — "when he saw him, he passed by on the other side." He instinctively shrunk; he would not even go near: "on the other side." Like many priests, like many people, he caught the scent of distant trouble, and kept clean out of it. No man of impulse he! a well-controlled person! the other side suited him better. He "passed by," and we see him recede up the road with dignified mien. He is on high church duty up at Jerusalem: these things must not stop him. Excuses of course he made to himself, for our great relief is in excuses and reasons. "To touch blood will make me unclean; I can't afford this delay; there is danger here, I must hasten on." So he goes.

And likewise a Levite came, a sacred person also; but he, "when he was at the place, came and looked on him." Some touch of nature drew him so far as to come and look, but no farther. I do not know which is worse, — to keep at a distance from the appeal of human need, or to be drawn near and then reject it.

"But a certain Samaritan—" At this point of the story there was a thrill of feeling in every Jewish heart that listened. What will the Samaritan do? You know about the Samaritans: they were mongrel Jews, with a mongrel Jewish religion, intensely hated by the Jew and intensely hating him. So of course there was a thrill of expectation. If the Jew is no brother to a Jew, if the sacred priest and Levite pass by, what will be said of the detested Samaritan? "But a certain Samaritan, as he journeyed, came where he was; and when he saw him, he had compassion on him, and went to him, and bound up his wounds, pouring in oil and wine, and set him on his own beast, and brought him to an inn, and took care of him. And on the morrow, when he departed,"—he stayed all night there with him, it seems,—"he took out two pence, and gave them to the host, and said unto him, Take care of him: and whatsoever thou spendest more, when I come again, I will repay thee."

Here the parable finishes. Observe the instinctive art in the form of this story,—especially in this, that most of its details are so sober and unromantic. No exaggeration, for example, no overwrought bad treatment on the part of the priest and the Levite, and on the other hand no overwrought excellence on the part of the Samaritan, no blackening of the bad or idealizing of the good, but all kept true to life. This wonderful Samaritan, the very model and transcendence of humanity for all time, says not one sentimental word; he is quiet, moderate, a very practical person, as thoroughly good people are apt to be, and he is altogether unlike what the ordinary novelist would make him. He says nothing beautiful; he does nothing profuse. He does not leave a purse of gold; he gives but two pence, — an adequate sum, no doubt, for present need, but nothing over; and if more should be required, he will repay it on his return.

It is just a picture of a worthy traveller on that road, a man nobly kind, but judicious and careful, — a picture reminding us of De Foe. Now, all this instinctive soberness keeps the story out of the region of romance, and gives a sense of reality to the substance of it. For the romantic, or imaginative, while it may seem to exalt virtue, makes it at once in a manner unreal and hard to practise, and the whole New Testament is a deep, unconscious protest against the romantic. It is not in the great splendid manner of the prophets, but quiet, because under a fine disguise the imagination is felt to be a real foe to the plain, pure heart of Christ, to the simplicity of righteousness. The good Samaritan is a character which might have been dipped in the hues and splendors of an angel; yet Christ's story makes him but a worthy, homespun man, all ideal glory veiled.

Here, then, is a picture of three neighbors, — the priest, the Levite, and the Samaritan; and here, as I said, the parable ends, Christ just asking the lawyer which he chooses. "Which now of these three, thinkest thou, was neighbor unto him that fell among the thieves?"

We must pause here, for this question is curious. The original inquiry of the lawyer was, "Who is my neighbor? — who are these persons whom you say, and the old law says, I must love as myself? how wide is my neighborhood? what number of objects must I take in?" — the real feeling in the heart being, "How few can demand my love? how may I make this terrible duty of loving everybody easy by restricting it?" The story in answer to this shows how widely a certain Samaritan felt, shows his beautiful mercy to his worst enemy, so that every heart, however prejudiced, must approve him and say, "Yes; this heart of unbounded love is the true neighbor, and every one who has need of his love and pity is their fit object;" and so the question is answered, not by showing how few I can confine my love to, how narrow I can draw the line, but showing that true love widens out to all want; that the neighborhood of man, as the neighborhood of God, spontaneously extends itself to all who need, be they foes or devils. O Jewish lawyer, you who are seeking out how little you can do and yet keep the commandment; you who try to obey it in some other way than through the wide heart of charity spreading everywhere, saying, "How narrow and selfish and hard can I be and yet get through?" you who seek to obey the law through some other way than love, which is the only fulfilling of the law, and doing it that you may inherit eternal life, and not at all that you care about your neighbor, — I tell you all you are wrong. I show you two pictures of sacred Jews like yourself, — one a priest, one a Levite, who have gone on in your way, in your spirit, and end by being neighbor to nobody but themselves, and leave the wounded brother dying in the highway; and I show you another picture of a Samaritan rescuing a Jew on the road, before whose love all partitions fall down, who, not thinking perhaps of his own eternal life at all, realizes need, and feels for it and goes out to it.

The chief point which remains to be considered is, that Christ pictures to Jews the true neighbor as a Samaritan. Dwell a moment there. Did you ever think what effect it would have had if, in telling us this story, he had made the neighborly man a Jew, — a Jew who was kind to a Samaritan? Though the lesson would still have been a good one, and taught the Jew to be catholic and pitiful, the effect would have been to sustain his pride and narrowness of heart: a great and hard sort of neighborliness, but at least it was a Jew who did it. Thus a wide pity, though in itself distasteful, might have been reluctantly accepted as a Jewish virtue, an act of grace from the proud nation to the world.

The true neighbor of whom Christ tells us is a Samaritan, and, according to all Jewish belief, half a heathen, half a heretic. It shows, first, Christ's most noble justice in judging enemies, and especially in judging heretics. The highest soul he pictures is in the worst heretic a Jew could think of, a Samaritan. What a lesson of burning shame to those ages which have judged a man, no matter what his heart was, entirely according to his belief! Believe with me and you are right; believe against me and you are wrong.

This significant fact of the Good Samaritan gives also a just sense of the spirit of Christ where otherwise there would be some doubt. There are some things which he says and does in the Gospels which look Jewish, and we are sometimes tempted to suppose that the portrait of the Son of God, being drawn by Jewish hands, has caught Jewish colors; but this parable clears all.

I wish we could even for a moment view Jesus Christ as he was. It would then need no doctrines of the Church to bring us all to our knees. Christ was a Jew, and in many respects the intensest spirit and affections of a Jew were in him; but he was so widely and beautifully "the Son of man," that he chooses the object of his admiration — the man who is to represent forever his own soul, the soul of the true neighbor — from among the "dogs and enemies" outside, and in the teeth of envenomed Jewish spite he sets a heretic up for love and reverence. No man nowadays can rightly conceive it; for no man can know the depth of prejudice to be overcome in order to reach such sublime elevation.

Our prejudices are even yet strong enough, but the prejudices of antiquity and of the East are worn smooth in these modern times; the gall is now almost made milk. The spirit of the Good Samaritan has passed from the lips of Christ into the atmosphere of the modern world, so that we do not know what the Jewish spirit was in the time of Christ. So we can never reproduce the force of the fact that Christ made his ideal good man a man who, as to half of the law, was a heretic. He depicts as the highest neighbor the man who can put every prejudice under his feet. Thus he makes the test of the true neighbor that he shall be a neighbor in spite of all that is against it. According to this, let us judge our own conduct. If we are kind to people who are pleasing to us, that is something, I don't deny it; but until we go much further and are kind in spite of personal, social, and religious prejudice, we are not the true neighbor. "For if ye love them which love you, what reward have ye? do not even the publicans the same? And if ye salute your brethren only, what do ye more than others?" You must be something much higher than this, even "the children of your Father which is in heaven: for he maketh his sun to rise on the evil and on the good, and sendeth rain on the just and on the unjust."

Who is my neighbor? Look at a Samaritan rescuing a Jew on the high-road. He lifts his worst enemy; he washes the wounds, he helps the bruised and broken man on to his own beast; he braves all the dangers of the road; and then goes his way, ready to do a like service to any one else. Who is my neighbor? Ask the South, the long-afflicted South, covered so long with the pall of sorrow, sprinkled by blood, — ask it to-day, after the scourges of war have afflicted it, ask it in this awful pestilence, "Who is your neighbor?" It will answer, "The noble men and women among us who do not desert us, the whole Howard Association, etc." Above all, perhaps it will answer, — God grant it may, — "The North, lately the enemy, lately the hated Samaritan, but now by its grand munificence lifting its bruised and broken Southern brother, washing his wounds, and ministering to his necessities. This is my neighbor." Last of all, if you will know your neighbor, look at the divine Samaritan, Christ. To the human heart he is a Samaritan with "no form nor comeliness," something we are averse to, a Samaritan to the proud human race; yet he is the neighbor, "the express image" of the returning God, of the redeeming God, who comes near to suffering humanity, who stoops to lift the wounded, and at the cost of his own blood exhibits, to each of us who need, the infinite mercy and neighborhood which is over all men.

XXIII.

WIDER VIEWS OF CHRISTIANITY.

There was a certain man in Cesarea, called Cornelius, a centurion of the band called the Italian band, a devout man, and one that feared God with all his house, which gave much alms to the people, and prayed to God always, etc. — ACTS x. 1-48.

THE subject is the opening of the mind of Peter, and with him, of the Jewish Christians generally (for he was the head, "the apostle of the circumcision"), to the world outside. Christianity among the Jews had two great stages of difficulty: First, when it aimed to enter the Jewish mind at all; Second, when it aimed to expand the Jewish Christian to the wide views of Christianity as it now is. In fact, these two things are one; namely, the full conversion of the Jews. But there were many gradations in this great passage from Judaism to Christianity. During the life of Christ some accepted him as a prophet, some as *the* prophet, and some, like Peter, "the Christ," advancing once so high as to say that he was "the Son of the living God."

But after all, the sense of who he was, and particularly of what his religion was, at the time of the crucifixion, was low and obscure, even to the topmost apostle. And after the Lord had risen, and the disciples were commissioned and illuminated, — after all this process they stood on the first stage only; there yet remained the second, namely, to reach the conviction that the Messiah was for all the world equally, that the Jew was no better than the Gentile, that the old sacred faith was to be put aside.

It was not so difficult to become a Christian as to believe that the Gentiles could become Christians. This was so unexpected, so contrary to every prejudice, even the best, that it seemed the wildest sacrilege, a mere infidel radicalism; and every personal feeling and habit, as well as the whole conscience of the Jew, rose up against it. Separation was the very soul of the laws of Moses. It was not, to be sure, peculiar to the Jews: it belonged to all antiquity, to the Greeks and Latins, but especially in the case of the Jew separation was his glory, and the Hebrew idea was, purity and strength through this exclusiveness; but the new doctrine of Christ was, purity and power through inclusiveness.

The old system, with its precious truths at its centre, derived its security from a sort of selfish rejection of the whole world. In the weakness of men as to idolatry, — for we are all naturally idolaters, and this tendency was then the master religious instinct of the world, — the truth and virtue of the unidolatrous religion were only saved by seclusion. Its challenge was, "Stand off!" But the new and more heavenly religion had a different heart; it had a new and strange spirit; it could afford to embrace all, and give itself to all, with an innocent fearlessness; it calculated not the dangers of scattering itself through a profane world, but, sublime in generosity and boldness, committed itself to all mankind.

So unlike this was the ancient system that even the Jewish vineyards could not be sown with divers seeds; for a mingling of seeds and of fruits, it was thought, would defile. The ox and the ass could not plough together, nor a man wear garments of divers materials, as woollen and linen. These every-day customs were emblems of the one great rule of the race, separation.

Here, however, one may say, "But Christianity is a development of Judaism." The answer is: This is true, but only in respect to the great germs planted in the old religion; not as to much in the institutions and spirit of the Mosaic law, and certainly not as to the way in which it was held. Christianity in its pure spirituality and in its openness, instead of being a development of Judaism, stands as its precise opposite: the one, of necessity, selfish and timid, — I mean comparatively so, — the other all disinterestedness and boldness and love; the one national, the other for the human race; the one for some ages and some places, the other for all time and for the whole world.

Such being the opposite spirit of the two religions, especially then, when God's old faith had dwindled into Pharisaism, they came together with the hiss and explosion of fire and water.

To such a people as the Jews, having been such for

ages, to preach communion, equality, was, next to blasphemy, the highest irreligion and the worst immorality. What! to put aside Abraham and the sacred race; to put aside Moses and the holy institutions, and to permit the awful temple to vanish as a mere architectural mass seen in the clouds at the setting of the sun; to profane the sacred Jewish land; to break down the walls of partition; to make the holy Jew unclean; to give up every Jewish hope, — in one word, that the Jew should cease to be a Jew, — why, this shocked patriotism and pride, abolished instincts, habits, and hopes, and, far more than all, shook the conscience to its foundations; violated, I may say, the bodily conscience as to cleanness and separation, and the mental conscience as to almost everything deemed sacred! Why, if you required the Greek to forget Athens, the Roman to deny Rome, the Hindu to profane his sense of caste, which is as deep as his life, — all this united would not be more than to ask the real Jew to cease to be a Jew!

We may think that at the time of which these chapters speak, when the Messiah was accepted, this great work of unjudaizing the Jew, unmaking him, had already been done. Not so. When the first disciples accepted the Messiah, this, so far from making them less Jews, only deepened many Jewish feelings and hopes, so that when the true character of Christianity developed itself, and they began to perceive that it was for the world, and that Judaism must be left behind, — then arose that profound struggle the history of which is one of the most interesting in the annals of the human mind. So astonishing was the idea that even Paul speaks of it as the mystery which hath been hid from ages, and is now made known,—an idea that is so foreign to the Jewish heart that God, who had great purposes to answer by this ancient religion, could not, from the foundations of the world, risk that even a whisper of this idea should be generally known, or his whole scheme would fly to pieces.

But as the Jew was thus of necessity narrow, why was it that the Christian seed should be planted in these strait iron vessels, where either the great tree must perish, or the vessel itself be shivered? Why was it not sown at first, and at once, upon the open soil of the world? Because the evidence, and much of the power of our revelation, is in this,—that it is a continuation, each part lending force to each through ages, and each stage preparing the heart for the next stage, advantages which a disconnected, an unprogressive revelation could never have. The principle on which God acted was growth, advance. Besides, great as were the obstacles to the full reception and spread of Christianity through Jewish hearts, yet in spite of that there was in the Jew the soil best fitted for it. Not only was his nature peculiarly fitted for the profound reception of religious ideas, but the previous stages of Hebrew education, while these had narrowed them, had yet made, at least some of them, ready, as no other souls were ever ready, for the reception, full apprehension, and propagation of this truth. Christianity needed Jewish souls as its apostles and teachers, and could nowhere else have found them. The mediation of this profound Jewish heart between Christ and the Gentiles, the manner in which we see it first used and then cast aside when it interfered with expansion, is a wonderful instance of Providence in history.

I say, when it interfered it was cast aside. And mark now, just at this point, before Judaism was divinely excluded, how imminent was the danger that, if the new religion were longer committed to the Jews and their prejudices, they would reduce and subordinate it, so as to make it but an enlightened Judaism. This was the immense risk; and any one who reads can see that Christianity was just on the edge of a great gulf, and if it had fallen into this there would have been, so far as we can see, thousands of years of delay and disaster to the race. Though this was avoided and Christianity saved, yet it is interesting to see how slowly and by what means it was done, — how Jewish Christians became at last Christians purely and only. The high mind of Stephen, the first martyr, gave the world, as it were, the first hint; then at his light the torch of Paul was kindled, or rather this wonderful creature Paul, who would himself have reached forward into all truth, caught, it is likely, the prompting of his first change of thought from Stephen; and so when Peter, the great head of the Jewish Christians, was still back in the twilight, Paul stood in the open day.

Just at this moment was the danger, when the enlightened Paul led forward the advanced wing of the church, and when Peter, still a Jew, headed the narrow Hebrew Christians, who hung far back, — just here was the danger that the Christian Church would be rent at its birth, that two ever-separating divisions would be made, Peter's ever sinking back more and more into the old, and Paul's ever moving, perhaps too rapidly and too far, into the new.

Here, then, was a moment worthy of a divine interposition. Without this, it seems impossible that the church of the circumcision could have been lifted out of that deep Jewish rut; and hence the events here recorded.

In this tenth chapter of Acts is a knot of miracles, beautifully blended, and pointing to one purpose. Cornelius at Cesarea, the representative of the Gentile world, and Peter at Joppa are both led as children by an invisible hand, and brought into communion and final brotherhood: the excellent Cornelius standing for all the world outside, — a world prepared and waiting and leaning forward for the light, — and Peter, the great repository of the light of truth which was as yet, we may almost say, burning in a dark lantern, induced now by a divine cogency to open the lantern and give the light.

You know the little history. Peter's heart was opened first by miracle, second by moral evidence.

As to this narrative, even if we in this age, so critical of miracles, are to judge of miraculous acts by the importance of the purpose, and by the tone and dignity of the acts themselves, we ought to be satisfied with these. The account is very beautiful, and without one disfiguring detail. The significant and poetic beauty of the great vessel, like a globe, as if representing the earth, filled with various creatures all made clean in the new order of things, and so the implied rebuke to Peter the regenerated Jew for keeping up the obsolete and now hateful distinction between the clean and the unclean animal, and much more between the peculiar race of men and all men, — this grand vessel, coming down from heaven to show the common birth of all, and taken back to the bosom of heaven as if all were there held dear, and this done three times, with rising emphasis, for the hungry Peter was eager to eat, but refused to do so, saying, with half-disgust perhaps, or with self-complacency, "Not so, Lord, for I have never eaten anything that is common or unclean;" the majestic voice replying, "What God hath cleansed, that call not thou common," — the scene vanishing the first time, but, to make sure of the effect, heaven opening yet twice more, and the voice repeating its mandate, — nothing could be more finely conceived. On the other hand, at Cesarea, a resplendent figure at the ninth hour stood "evidently" before Cornelius, and said, "Thy prayers and thine alms are come up for a memorial before God."

Observe, God, who at Joppa was declaring to Peter the cleanness of every good man, here at Cesarea was acting out the principle towards Cornelius, and so making the one transaction at Cesarea to vindicate the other at Joppa.

Take notice, in the next place, of this important fact; namely, that in convincing and persuading Peter the moral evidence, as to the heart of the good Cornelius, is added to the supernatural evidence. The vision opened Peter's mind, to be sure, and when the messenger came he went to Cornelius; but it was not until he saw the good man and his household gathered reverentially before him, and heard the humble and devout words, "Now therefore are we all here present before God, to hear all things that are commanded thee of God," — then at last came the full sense that the Gentile heart was not common, that this man was better than a child of Abraham, being a son of God; and so, at once and honestly, "Peter opened his mouth, and said, Of a truth I perceive that God is no respecter of persons; but in every nation he that feareth him, and worketh righteousness, is accepted with him." At one bound Peter overleaps the limits of the Jew, and goes far beyond many even now.

Some writers speak of Peter as naturally bigoted. He was a sincere and genuine Jew, — not of the very largest thought, as Paul, and not to be judged by so high a standard; but still his was an open, teachable, and intrepid spirit. If his age is remembered — a fact of the very greatest importance in judging of such a matter — his forwardness to accept views radically new will surprise any one who knows mankind, will surprise as much as that vast conversion of Saul to Paul. He was firm in his beliefs, certainly; and it is a remarkable fact that God chose such instructors as these two men, both so intense in their convictions as to be wrenched out of them only by miracles. It shows us how God values earnestness, and how well he saw that these two Jews, who lived in a burning heat of Judaism, would, when once converted, pour other flames, purer, but not less fervid, into the world, — would burn, in fact, as that fire which the Lord said he was about to "send on the earth." Yes; once set on fire by the real truth, they burned as vividly along the rim of the widest circle as they had done at the narrow Jewish centre.

Call not then such a soul as Peter's the soul of a bigot, and iron-bound. Was *he* not open, who, of all the earth, first felt the deep appreciation of Jesus, — who first stood forth and said, "Thou art the Christ"? Yes; his heart was open, and his soul intrepid. But his fault, his weakness, as is always the case, lay near his virtue. He was all in the present feeling; and so, under any new impression, he was ever liable to extreme reactions. The man who yesterday led the circumcision, to-day said, "In every nation he that feareth him, and worketh righteousness, is accepted with him." But to-morrow this very man — as we read in the Epistle to the Galatians — was openly rebuked by Paul for yielding once more to his sympathies for the Jews, and possibly to his old Jewish prejudices, and refusing to eat with the Gentile brethren. "I withstood him to his face," says Paul, "for he was to be blamed."

The man who first recognized the Lord, then openly and meanly denied him, "I know not the man,"—the man who saw here so clearly the great vessel descending unto him, who felt that God had stretched out the lines of his household as wide as the encircling skies, yet shrinks from opposing the prejudices of his Jewish brethren; and though he was naturally the bravest man in the New Testament record, yet the only acts of individual cowardice among the disciples there set down are the acts of the brave Peter.

Here, in these chapters, is the grand encouragement to an unprejudiced and tolerant spirit,—the very spirit of Christ, which is union and not disunion, brotherhood not enmity, and which puts down all small causes of separation between man and man. The rule is for us also,—"what God hath cleansed, that call not thou common." He hath cleansed whatever he hath created; whatever he has sanctioned in the natural world as good enough to be his creature, whatever in society and usage he has established and sanctioned (sin and crime always apart), that is good enough to be respected by us. This simple rule sweeps away at once the differences of race, of language, of customs, of occupations, of the orders and classes in social life,—all those myriad walls which shut out the sympathies of one class, nay, one individual, from another. A common fatherhood makes common children.

I mean not to preach political equality (that depends on circumstances), or social equality, or any individual equality; for Nature puts her ban on all such folly. Does she make any two things equal? Is not her whole kingdom subordination? Is not that the spirit of the gospel? Yet it is also perfect brotherhood of heart, animating and dignifying all, — the lofty willingly coming down from their seat to raise the beggar from the dust, — "the brother of low degree" rejoicing in the elevation of him that is above him. "Orders and degrees jar not with liberty, but well consist," said the great Puritan, John Milton. So, resisting all mere levelling, yet, on the other hand, to use personal or social or political advantages selfishly, to stand apart in our prejudices, to oppress the deserving, to harden our hearts against any of the children of God, — what is all this but to erect again all those devil-built walls of partition which the Lord has thrown down "with the breath of his mouth"?

Are you Christians? What is the meaning of that? "Into what were ye baptized?" Into a common sonship to God, into a common redemption by Christ, into a common heart, into fraternity with man, calling nothing but sin and meanness, in high or low, "common or unclean." For remember there is one Redeemer and Elder Brother who hath laid his hand upon us all, and I cannot hope for his forgiveness if I forgive not my brother.

Then, as to my religious convictions. Wherever in doctrine an imperious dogma is, or a putting of intellectual conclusions before charity and brotherhood, there is the spirit of the Jew. Yes, though I justly hold my religious convictions to be of costly value, and though I must strive for the truth at any sacrifice, yet if my brother, whom I see of as good life as myself, or better, whom I see to be as earnest for truth as I am, if he differs with me shall I rule him to be but " an heathen man and a publican "? Shall I call him " unclean " whom God hath cleansed? What is the central test of the Church, given by God; what points it out to the world? " By this shall all men know that ye are my disciples, if ye have love one to another." Human nature takes any excuse to make a separation, and prides itself upon it: " I have never eaten anything that is common or unclean." After the Christian world has been baptized into so divine a unity, into the belief of one God and Father of all, and one Lord who is over all, and who was crucified for all, and one Spirit, and one general temper, is it not time we should subordinate such differences as are not essential to Christian life to that beautiful spirit, spoken of by Paul, which " hopes all and believes all "? And while we stand firm for all truth, let us remember that in the great vessel of the world variety and multiplicity are allowed; " all manner of four-footed beasts of the earth, and wild beasts, and creeping things, and fowls of the air."

We still need the lesson. The old times, to be sure,

are past, when the very tolling of the church bells seemed to be a tolling for battle. But even now, side by side with a false tolerance, — which only seems liberal because it is indifferent, — are also the remains, with some persons certainly, of a blind, unchristian prejudice against all not of their own immediate household. These overlook the injury done to the common faith for the sake of some special views, and really seem to lose the sense of a common Master and a common salvation and a common future in any petty difference.

But do not misunderstand; do not think I am preaching church equality. I am not a believer in equality, but in distinctions and superiorities of all sorts. Yet when I am found expelling what Christ accepts, refusing one of the least of these his brethren, magnifying distinctions, and belittling the things which identify, then I may be sure of one thing, — that that is the precise reverse of Christ and his temper, and that if I have not his temper I am none of his. "He that is not against us is for us," was his divine declaration; and his was the voice which majestically announced to his servant Peter, "What God hath cleansed, that call not thou common."

XXIV.

THE DEPTHS OF SATAN.

And no marvel; for Satan himself is transformed into an angel of light. — 2 COR. xi. 14.

AT Corinth there were, it seems, as we should expect, "deceitful workers," who gave out that they were the apostles of Christ; and they not only pretended to the look and air of apostles, but such was their skill in hypocrisy, the depth of their deceitful working, that they actually seemed better apostles than Paul himself. But this was no marvel, says Paul, for Satan himself, the head malignant of the creation, the worst of the set, appeared to be an angel of light; for the depth of his mysterious deceit was such that he was actually transformed to suit his purposes.

"I marvel not, then," said the deep apostle, "when I see evil looking as good, because I know that the centre of evil itself, the father of it, the blot in Nature, — even he may cover himself with grace and name himself the Son of the Morning, and come forward with a shining face among the sons of God."

I have nothing to say as to the personality of this fountain of evil. It is sufficient to know that there is a dark power pervading Nature and spirits; and, knowing that, let us fix our eyes upon this fact about it, — its indescribable deceptiveness. It were better to say, this fact which is at its heart, and which is its life; for evil is deception, and has no existence apart from deception. It gets all its power by looking another thing than it is.

We know that the apostle speaks of evil as "sitting in the temple of God, showing himself that he is God," or, as Milton expresses it, "with godlike imitated state." It is a grand and universal mimicry of God or goodness, from the lowest of the forms of good up to the highest. If we were to go through every species of evil that has ever seduced man or angel, the moment of its power would be found to be when it wore a fair mask upon its face; and the more heavenly the look the mask has, the subtler and more resistless is its charm. If we get at the very core of things evil, it is always an ugly and disgusting core; but around it are often the finest shows and the richest aroma of the creation; and so in borrowed garments it sits in the midst of the temple of God, showing itself as God. All false religions, indeed, in us Christians or in heathendom, are but some heavenly spirit leavening a satanic mass.

Some philosophical minds defend this blending and hiding of evil under good, because they say — which is no doubt true — that it relieves the brutality of the evil and saves the conscience. But I answer: first, it makes the introduction of evil easy; secondly, it gradually lets down the mind to any depth. There is a celebrated saying of Burke, in allusion to the splendid vice of the

French court, that "vice lost half its evil by losing all its grossness;" which is strongly defended by the acute mind of Sir James Mackintosh, on the principle that all disguise is a limitation upon vice. These excellent and illustrious persons did not intend a pernicious statement; but a maxim of this sort can be defended only through not adverting to the distinctions just noticed.

Pure iniquity shocks; but where some good affection recommends it, then it becomes an angel of light, and serves as a beautiful shell to cover in the satanic centre; and it is a fearful fact that the deepest sensibilities often serve to make the heart the easier victim of its power. It was the woman's nature that fell first, as the Bible records. Why? Because of her weakness. But wherein the weakness? In the very source of her strength,— the more vivid sensibility,— not only the sense that the fruit was "pleasant to the eyes," but the dazzle of the thought that it would elevate, that it was "to be desired to make one wise,"— this dazzle it was that made her first in the transgression. And so it ever is with her. And so it ever is with strong feelings and powerful imaginations. I mention this to the young, to all, as a trumpet of warning.

Now, of this deception our life is crowded with instances. The holy affection of parent for child covers up and to some extent justifies to the parent the most arrant selfishness as respects him and his. The indispensable virtue of prudence, the necessity for the honorable energy which foresees and provides, conceals at this moment from whole masses of men their distrust in God, their reliance on the most unreliable things, their greedy grasp of the world. So the heartless conceit and selfishness of ambition chooses for itself the fairest names and forms to cover it, — glory, patriotism, etc. Wherever we look, war, letters, science, high place in the State, — all gather a thousand artificial and some real grandeurs to cover over with angelic light the various Satans which lie powerful at the centre. That old sorcerer who once spread out to the purest eye of Christ the kingdoms of the world still covers with his cloth of state all the sordid objects of life; he still calls selfish grasping honorable aspiration, and the harlotries of vanity shine with the name and as if with the lights of true glory.

Strip off these fair names and coverings, and we have below — what? Look into the heart of Napoleon, look through into the very heart of that most imperial of all forms which ever awed the world, and what do you see there? A man says he is seeking public good, wealth, power, for honorable ends, or maybe self-culture, or a noble truth and beauty, and so he covers himself with these shining names; but if you look under the drapery you will find a contemptible little idol, as deformed often as a Hindu god. Nay, every best and purest affection, the love of man to woman, faithfulness to duty, to religious truth, we so abuse as to allow under their holy shelter passions, defects, which would blush in the open daylight.

I do not say we deliberately put ourselves under this deception. For the most part this is not so. We are drawn away scarcely conscious of the delightful lie. But the man alive to duty always detects or may detect the cheat. He may; but the song in his ears is a fair song, and the eyes are half willing to close, and the enchanted world is welcomed, for it seems fairer than the common daylight. It is so delightful to look at inferior things in this superior way, to cover them with fair names, to call, for example, our weak, self-indulgent compassion to the poor charity, or to call our ostentation charity, or to call our gross calculations for self charity, — for "the coward to say he is a wary man, or for the miser to say he is frugal." This angel of light so beautifully adorns it all that we close our eyes on the devilish legerdemain.

I am a proud man, or I am a great self-seeker, or of a bitter temper, with many personal grudges. Now, I may wreak all these tempers, not only without danger, but to great advantage, under the cover of interest to my party or my set. If I am called a Christian, how stirring my public benevolences, so long as they are public! how keen am I for the truth! — that is, perhaps, for certain prejudices or superstitions which I have built up between me and my brother and call truth, though it is such truth as will not keep the unity of the Spirit, and breaks the golden bond of peace. Many a church partisan feels covered all over with the armor of a champion of the light; and yet what is he but a poor deluded creature, working the works of Satan?

So through the whole. There is not one evil which wears not a face as of a twin brother to some good. When we are making excuses and explanations to ourselves for a course we are bent on taking, then the good gifts of our mind are perverted to smooth the way to sin, and we give occasion to that fine satiric sentence, "So convenient a thing is it to be a reasonable creature, for it enables one to find or make a reason for everything one has a mind to."

The only sort of science, perfection in which is absolutely required, is the science of knowing "the depths of Satan." Until we learn more of these depths, let us take this one rule: When there is any tinge or doubt of evil, fear it most where it comes most warm and natural and lovely. Or sometimes when it comes more sacred still, —

> "Breathing like sanctified and pious bonds,
> The better to beguile."

In all these cases, fear it. "Abhor that which is evil;" though it be as lofty in stature as a god, though its face be living with charms as if fresh out of heaven, though it be covered with imperial honors, "the kingdoms of the world and the glory of them," — abhor it!

Discriminate; prove all things; try them by the model of Christ, by his divine rules, or better still by his divine temper. I know nothing else in books, nothing in men's heads or hearts that can teach us how surely to detect Satan. Christ is the one who himself was utterly undeceived, and who looked at all things as they are. Study him, catch his views, get that spirit of most disinterested, humble love for God and the interests of man, and every form of the base and selfish will start up from its myriad disguises, discovered to its last fibre, naked and hideous.

XXV.

THE OFFICE OF JUDGMENT.

In the image of God created he him. — GEN. i. 27.

IN many aspects was man intended to be in the image of God; and they are all interesting and high, and are the claims of our nature to a natural nobility, until we become in part self-degraded and self-deposed. Man was intended as the visible representative of God as "the Judge of all the earth." We are all, by the very constitution of our spirits, intended to be set in the earth for judgment.

This fact has been felt by all men throughout their history; but it is most singular to see how the feeling has shown itself. It has not come clearly out in the consciousness of men as a fact true of themselves, true of all men (as it is), but true of kings or patriarchs or divine men only. At the time of the Hebrew patriarchs it was felt that theirs was a peculiar power, of adjudging a blessing or curse, — a judicial power, which sent good or evil down into the life. So it was felt as to prophets and diviners such as Balaam. The feeling of men was that such a power of judging did exist on earth, but that it could only belong to the leaders, the old men, the prophets, the men nearer God.

So, in the same way of thinking, throughout common history the profane mass has been denied all the eminent glories of humanity, that they might be gathered as aureolas around a few select heads. While the simple truth is that the title of all men to judge is just according to the degree in which God has given them a just heart and mind; just in proportion to that, they share with him by a natural title in his office of judgment, — Christ the supreme judge, after him those who are most like him. But men have ever stripped themselves, as a race, of the finest distinctions of their humanity; and the reason of this has been, that the mass of human kind until lately were in the unconscious humility of children as to themselves, but as to their great ones they could believe anything; their sacred ones seemed to them (in their reverential imaginations) to share the mysterious lights and powers of God.

Of course, all this was based in some cases on a real ground of truth; namely, that some chosen men are somewhat more in the image of God than others. But the same feeling operates throughout history, even where the higher men are really not higher at all. The world has all along bowed down to the decrees of conventional orders of men, artificial classes, Brahmins and priests for example, and their voices only have stood for the judgments of God.

But the gospel of Christ broke boldly for the first time upon this delusion, and proclaimed that all men of the Spirit, that is, all true souls, are kings and priests unto God; that judgment, the power to "open and shut," receive and reject, bless and curse, belongs to be sure eminently to chosen men, but belongs also to every faithful man. This was the true spirit of the gospel.

The Christian Church, however, received this great truth but for a moment, and almost immediately ran back to its old superstitions about leading or official men, and deposited the precious duties and rights of humanity in the hands of an order. So what was at first in the Christian Church a power of divine judgment, given to all, but especially and in an eminent sense to apostles and leaders (because to their illuminated hearts it specially belonged), this power, the "power of the keys" of the kingdom of heaven, to open and to shut, to say what man or what truth should come in or be shut out, to absolve or condemn, — this power gradually and ever since has been grasped and used by the priesthood of that very ancient and powerful church, the Church of Rome.

But let me do that priesthood no injustice. Its priestly powers were not so much grasped by them as devolved upon them by the condition of the mass in Europe from that day to this. The world of Christians in ignorant humility, losing sight of their own claims and duties as born representatives of God upon earth, to judge and guide themselves and others, have willingly yielded up this heavenly prerogative, anxious to get rid of the responsibility of themselves. Yes, and not merely the ignorant, but intelligent people, from among ourselves (so deeply seated is this weakness), pass, even to-day, into the Church of Rome for this very purpose, to discharge themselves of all judgment, to unman themselves; for it is the true and only manhood of man to continue in the image of God, of which this great office of judgment is one aspect. The high thing is always the hard thing; and this high office of judgment which requires at every step that the whole conscience and will be awake, has been gladly given away and got rid of.

But we Protestants at least do better, — a little, but not much better. Men have never been high enough yet to be truly men. Are not our judgments of truth, for example, made for us by others? Who has established theology and bound it upon Protestantism, but a few scholastic heads? Yet this is pardonable. It is not pardonable, however, that the Christian heart should not learn to judge from its own self at least of the great aspects of truth, and much more to judge Christian practice and morals.

But one thing more, and worst of all, as to our Protestant boast of private judgment. Protestantism, in claiming the right of judgment for the individual, has made one egregious mistake. It has at least permitted, if it has not encouraged, a mistake as to where in human nature the seat of judgment is. Not in the cold head, judging the letter of the Bible, — not there is the seat of judgment. In the cultivated spiritual soul, in the pure heart, brought under the influence of Bible truth, there is the light which judges of all spiritual light, the *imperium in imperio*,— the top of judgment. Now, the insufficient emphasis of this fact has gradually turned much of Protestant thinking into a mere intellectual criticism; and mere intellect, judging of things spiritual, is scepticism! So we see on the one hand that the Church of Rome has usurped, in the interests of a class, the judgment God gave to all men; and we see on the other hand that Protestantism, while seeming to reassert the rights of individual judgment, has done so in part imperfectly and in part mistakenly.

But next, we ought to be not only judges in this general sense, but more specifically judges of the character of one another in the ordinary sense. We are to be judges of one another, carefully, to be sure, because of our ignorance, benignly because of our brotherhood, but still to judge one another and to "spread plenty of justice and equity upon the earth." I know that the best and most judicial men (aware of their own infirmities, aware how much the pure light of judgment which comes down from God into the spirit is dimmed) feel instinctively that they would gladly put away all judgment as to their fellows. As Saint Paul said, "I judge nothing before the time, until the Lord [the king of judges] come." He meant that his tendency was, in cases of doubt, not to be arbitrary and foolishly certain, but gladly, and wherever he could, to commit all judgment to Christ; but such cases apart, Saint Paul himself declares that man is gifted with the highest powers of judgment. "Know ye not that ye shall judge angels?" and as a matter of fact he himself exercised continually the office of a high judge, and by no title but because of the judicial spirit that was in him. And so of all men who share in the same spirit; judgment is asked of them, benign but real, the weight of their approval or disapproval. This is one of the demands upon us as human, as made in the image of God; we cannot put it off; "we are appointed thereunto," — appointed to acquit or condemn as one of the delegated judges of the earth.

This is true. Yet as a matter of fact what do we find? We find a large body of men seize judgment gladly, but only that they may use it selfishly or malignantly, rushing to decisions concerning their fellow-creatures in a bold, selfish, and ignorant spirit, and under the guise of judges taking the place of executioners. The lips of men and women made sweet and sacred to truth and justice are poisoned and black with wrong. This is one side. On the other, there is a class of good but falsely conscientious people who decline the office of judging altogether. Did not the Lord say, "Judge not, and ye shall not be judged"? Yes, to be sure those divine lips spake that; but of course he meant unjust judges and overweening condemnations. It would be better, I think, if the words stood, not "judge not," but "censure not, and ye shall not be censured." Whose voice sounds with a louder and nobler ring of judgment than his? Not any. I know that he censures, but I know that his kindness, while it suffused and limited his justice, never destroyed it; if it had, his mercy would be a curse.

But you have no right to be judging others, you say. Yes, but you have; and more than a right, you have a duty. The only question is, how you shall perform it. The world wants justice. The earth mourns and languishes for the want of it. Human affairs need it, individual men need it, and the hearts of some men are half consumed in the thirst for justice. "I want but justice," they say. Yes, and the way the world is going on, you will want it. Many people will give you scandal and censure but omit the justice, while some good men stand by and will not interfere. "The world wants justice," I repeat; and the only question is how, in what spirit, right-hearted men shall speak it and act it.

Now, to know this rightly, we must know that God's judges must have righteous ends in view, and judge without spleen or selfishness. That is first. We must imitate the dignity of the public justice as we see it practised in our solemn tribunals. We must not be hasty, we must demand the evidence, grounds more pertinent than gossip, or else entirely refuse judgment; and in all points we must let our justice lean towards equity, and our equity lean towards mercy.

Besides, two things are demanded of every judge, — personal purity and fearlessness. Our judgment must be as pure as an act of religion, and as fearless, with no private meanness or unbrotherhood at the bottom of our hearts. Fearlessness in the pure judge is especially to be admired; especially, because ordinary people are so cowed by power and influence, so cowed by the slanderer, that justice is kept back through fear. Most strange to say that the unjust men of the world frighten men so much by their calumnies that justice is often silent, and even sometimes pays blackmail to its enemy. I have known, perhaps you have known, whole communities where the worst of slanderers have been treated, if not with respect yet with particular care; just as in some countries the serpent, and in Japan the fox, because supposed to be animals inhabited by demons, are on that account consecrated and worshipped, and enjoy the best of the land, — really devil-worship. The just and fearless judge, who puts under his feet the fear of the slandering newspaper or slandering man or woman, deserves a monument.

Finally, we are appointed to be judges of ourselves; and the great rule of this judgment is to be merciful to others but severe to ourselves; for selfish as we are, it is always safe to deduct largely from our indulgence towards ourselves and to add largely to our indulgence towards others. There is an instance of this sort of modesty and equity of heart in the private journals of Sir James Mackintosh, to which I am glad to recur. He says, speaking of a certain person: " This gentleman has, I think, a distaste for me, which I believe to be natural to all his family. I think the worse of nobody for such a feeling. Indeed, I often feel a distaste for myself. I am sure I should not esteem my own character in another person. It is more likely I should have disrespectable or disagreeable qualities than that such a person should have an unreasonable antipathy for me." Now, here is the veritable Christian spirit in the judgment of self. The scales of pure justice this man carried into the public courts of his country, but he carried other scales into the judgments of his own heart, — scales swayed and tipped by modesty, by generosity, and by a fine Christian honor. Generosity, then, is the rule in all questions of self towards others. And then, last, as to that still higher judgment, — the judgment of self before God. We need no generous measures, only consciousness of self as it is. I must ask myself simply, What am I? what thoughts do I harbor? what ends do I pursue? what do I love and hate? I am a creature; am I grateful and humble to the dust before my Creator? I am redeemed from death; am I thankful and trustful and obedient? What is the fact? And remember what you candidly say of yourself to-day and here God will say of you, a little farther on, at the great judgment-seat. " Beloved, if our heart condemn us, God is greater than our heart, and knoweth all things. Beloved, if our heart condemn us not, then have we confidence toward God."

We have glanced now, only glanced, at the whole range and solemnity of the judgment given to man as made in the image of God the Judge. I have said that we are appointed judges of truth, — we, and not somebody else, however high and venerable. I have said that we are appointed judges of our fellows, to announce judgment towards them, to set right the wrongs of the world, yet to do it in mercy. I have said we are set for the judgment of self, to rehearse the coming judgment-day of God. Who then recognizes his great place as judge? Who remembers that the constitution of his nature and the example of Christ call him "to do justice and to love mercy;" to judge, but in the Lord's purity, and in his sweetness and mercy, — judging others as we ourselves may hope to be judged?

XXVI.

GOD'S REBUKE OF APPEARANCES.

When the morning was come, all the chief priests and elders of the people took counsel against Jesus to put him to death. — MATT. xxvii. 1.

TO any thoughtful person, whatever his belief, there is indescribable interest in the scenes just preceding the death of Christ. The closing of his story, it seems, was meant to be the most impressive record of this world. I mean to speak of this great scene, excluding everything else and everything higher, with but one thought mainly in view, — God's rebuke of appearances, — as a vast illustration of those words which the Lord himself once uttered: "Judge not according to the appearance, but judge righteous judgment."

If we consider this scene as it was looked at then, and as it was in fact, we shall see, as we never saw before, the rebuke of appearances, first in showing how guilt may look like virtue, and virtue like guilt. There at that moment was virtue itself, it would seem, in the form of high accusers, standing for God and his law, and ready to vindicate that great cause. Who were they? They were the high dignitaries of the Jewish people, engaged for religion and order against innovation, the venerable protectors of the sacred past. There also was guilt, in the form of a man accused and finally condemned. He seemed to be a singular person, for a time popular with the mass, but one who could not long be popular with any mass; besides, he was detested by the great heads, for his views threatened the comfort and respectability of the better classes, and indeed the existing order of things.

There he stands quite friendless, obviously guilty and accursed; for are not the rulers against him? is not public opinion against him? are not the ardor and cries of the multitude joined with the gravity of the rulers and the aged, — the one vitalizing, the other consecrating the cause? So the man before them is obviously ignominious; their hearts feel it, and he looks so to their very eyes. Such is the color of power, which can make the blue of the heavens take a different tint.

So he looked to them, while they looked to themselves in every point pure and respectable persons. They went not into the Roman "judgment-hall, lest they should be defiled, but that they might eat the passover." Indeed, so pure, and with this blood upon their hands! They were also grateful for God's deliverances; at least they religiously kept the passover, and at this moment, when about to eat the paschal lamb, whose blood saved the early Hebrews, they make ready to destroy that other lamb, "which taketh away the sins of the world."

See these merciful, scrupulous, devout, theological Jews, — see how sacred their guilt appears; and see the very highest, holiest, looking so low in the opinion of the moment that every man can spit upon him, and his assigned place is between two crucified thieves. They forget their own history, — the few pure and high against the many low; they take for granted that what is on top is best; theirs is the old feeling which slew the prophets, namely, this man is not according to our ideas, therefor he is wrong, hateful, fit to be killed. We know something of Jesus Christ: there he is, judged and felt not fit to live. We know this Jewish mob, these scribes and Pharisees: there they all are, swelling in the consciousness of virtue and virtuous indignation, vindicating religion and saving their country. There were no doubt secret misgivings among them; and woe unto the man who does not listen when the soul hints he is wrong!

There were three parties on this occasion who claimed to have knowledge. The Jewish leaders first: "We have a law." They claimed to know truth. Pilate also claimed to know. When Christ spoke of "the truth," Pilate turned away with a sneering doubt, and said, "What is truth, — that is, who claims to know? Have not all the minds of all the schools left it where they found it, — in endless uncertainty?" Here spoke the sad result of all Greek and Roman thought, — doubt: "We know only that we can't know." Pilate felt that he was a master in this matter, that he had reached the glorious end of all philosophy, and took his seat on nothing.

The Jew was proudly certain that his half-truths or his falsehoods were God's truth; the Roman was proudly certain that no man knew anything about it; and between these two the thought of the world was then divided. But there was a third Person here. He stood in the presence of the two august authorities in the domain of thought, and of all the results they had reached, and quietly claimed that the truth was with him. "Then Pilate entered into the judgment-hall again, and called Jesus, and said unto him, Art thou the King of the Jews? Jesus answered, My kingdom is not of this world. . . . Pilate therefore said unto him, Art thou a king then? Jesus answered, Thou sayest that I am a king. To this end was I born, and for this cause came I into the world, that I should bear witness unto the truth." A king, but not of this world, — a witness unto the truth, and all they who are of the truth will range themselves under him.

Contrast the imposing Jewish truth, the learning and refinement of the rabbis and doctors; contrast the imposing philosophic doubt of the Greek and Roman world, — contrast all this with the quiet voice of a seeming criminal just about to be crucified, who said, amid sneers, that he was the king of the truth; and then remember where Jewish and Roman truth is to-day, — antiquated, dwarfed, swept with the dust into a corner, — and remember that to-day the thought of this criminal shapes all virtue; that in the line of his truth the world runs and must run; that on the certainty of his convictions we stand as on our only rock; that if his voice were silent, the invisible world would sink back, if not into total darkness, at least into shadows; the face of God the Father of men would unshape itself into an idol, perhaps into a monstrous nothing, — no God; that if his voice were silent, the whole earth would unchristianize itself, its moral promise wither, and the human heart itself die in the human bosom.

I see here the Jewish prince, Herod, "with his men of war," — Herod, the representative of that line of kings who succeeded to the very kingship of God; here stands Pilate in his judgment-hall, representing the imperial might and the imperial law of Rome; with them stand a unique set of men, rulers and priests and scribes, representing perhaps the oldest, certainly the most singular and by far the highest and most sacred religion of the world, — properly, indeed, its only religion, — in the background the wonderful temple of that religion; all this stands here, and all this is at the moment supported by the popular will of a nation, by the masses of the Jewish people.

This is imposing, to be sure. This is the appearance; but what is beneath it? As to the prince of the Jewish people, he is but a poor worldling and trifler, and plays his high part as judge by using the occasion to satisfy his curiosity and to amuse his luxurious leisure; for when he "saw Jesus he was exceeding glad, because he had heard many things of him, and he hoped to have seen some miracle done by him." As to the Roman governor representing Roman justice, — the wisest and most impartial justice the world had ever known, — what does he? He is awed and superstitiously impressed by the presence of Christ, says, "I find no fault in him," yet from selfish fears and selfish interests yields, and " delivers him to be crucified." And as to the imposing heads of the church of God, whose law was "to do justice and judgment," so mean and malignant and cruel were their hearts, that it was as if the sacred robe of the high priest covered a monster. Yet how high it all was! And as for Him, — what is he? A thing "despised and rejected." Yet how infinitely different the fact!

Again: I see here how deceptive are the appearances of shame and of glory; for manifestly it was true once, and may be true again, that just in that thing where the stain of ignominy seems blackest a peculiar honor may come to shine.

Nothing in the last scenes of Christ affects my own mind so much as the shame and mocking, — mocking so keen and contemptuous, — a depth of malignant irony such as I know nowhere else. "Herod with his men of war set him at naught, and mocked him, and arrayed him in a gorgeous robe." Except Pilate, they all mocked, — Herod, the soldiers, the spectators under the cross, the priests, — all. They mocked his kingship, and the idea of his power. "They that passed by reviled him, wagging their heads, and saying, Thou that destroyest the temple, and buildest it in three days, save thyself;" and it was reserved, last of all, for the chief priests with the scribes to mock. I see here, also, how poor are our ideas of success and defeat. At that moment all the world had declared for wrong, and Holiness and Love hung nailed to the cross. The few poor friends of Christ "forsook him and fled;" and that hour was so awful to them that they felt the earth shake beneath their feet, and darkness was over the whole land from the sixth to the ninth hour. It was certainly the hour and power of darkness. The crowd dispersed; the priests, much pleased, went back to the temple, the governor to his palace. Jesus was dead, and Satan had sat down on the throne of the world.

It was finished, then, in the blackness of darkness, and just then the universal dayspring broke in the east. From that moment he took, and will take forever his place. The Being most ignominious, most mocked, becomes forever — on that continent, on this, to you, to me, and to the child born thousands of years hence — our Master, our Lord, our Lord God; and to him every knee shall bow; and his blood and sorrows shall cleanse and heal all sinful and broken hearts forevermore; his name the Saviour of the world. And those Jews, howling like wolves upon his path, — as they recede from us we see them covered with shame and hissing, and his blood, alas! sprinkled upon them and upon their children. So in the great magic of Providence the pictures of false glory grow black, its crowns wither, while the image of holiness and love, marred and stained, is set upon a throne which is "from everlasting to everlasting."

This whole scene I consider as a rebuke of false appearances; for here is exhibited such a profound contrast between reality and show, between what is and what seems, that we almost see an invisible person pointing his unmoving finger at the whole. I see here on the grandest scale such complicated irony as I know not of in any record, — the irony of facts; that is, facts so dramatically organized as to present the most gigantic godlike contempt of the false grandeurs, wisdom, dignity of man. Man needs humbling; the mean greatness of the false heart needs to be exposed; and this is done at the cross of Christ. How it came to be thus done, I can only explain in one way, — that it was a purposed, deliberate, divine mock of wrong and false men. God is accustomed so to speak and act in the Bible. Why should we be shocked, then, that the divine vengeance, which shines lurid about every wrong deed, should speak most keenly at the death of Christ?

Shall the solemn scorn at the littleness and blindness of sin, which we may see everywhere in history, — in our own lives, indeed, if we look closely, — shall this not be seen also in that one awful history? There the very ideal of wrong, covered with power, confronted the meek and beautiful Spirit of heaven, towered over him, scorned him, ironized him, put a reed in his hand for a sceptre; and shall not the Divine Justice at that supreme moment come forth and reverse the whole, and present this proud and cruel show to everlasting shame? Yes; a divine Spirit so ordered, and there stands the grand retributive mocking. Pilate thought, no doubt, it was his own sneer, when full of contempt he wrote a title, in Hebrew, and Greek, and Latin, "Jesus of Nazareth the King of the Jews;" but his sneer is lost in the godlike, unspeakable irony which is behind it. Who does not see divine indignation coming out boldly everywhere, and sculpturing itself in eternal images of scorn? Why, it arrests one almost as much as if God himself had stepped upon the scene.

What is the purpose in all this? The purpose to shame the soul, — the high and tyrannous and mean soul. This on the one hand, while on the other there is an opposite and just as clear a purpose, — to let the most touching love be so cruelly outraged, to let every grace and nobleness of Christ be so treated, made so abject to the eye, spit upon, ridiculed, harried, crushed out of life, and cast away as refuse, that from under all this its inmost glory might be forced to the surface, its fragrance of divine patience and pity and boundless loveliness be crushed into the atmosphere, that we might see there, standing side by side, sin and its heavenly contrast, midnight and morning; and so that we all with an immortal repugnance might be driven from the one, and with an immortal drawing might turn to the other.

XXVII.

THE SPIRIT OF CHRIST.

Lift up your heads, O ye gates; and be ye lifted up, ye everlasting doors; and the King of glory shall come in. — Ps. xxiv. 7.

I TAKE the spirit of Christ to be the perfect rule, not only of individual life, but of society, of business, of government, and of all law; for the spirit of Christ is the ideal of humanity. It is the perfect soul in all its relations public and private, full of justice, fairness, wisdom, and self-sacrifice. But that full spirit of Christ is kept out, defeated, or at least limited by various necessities, but chiefly by human selfishness and ignorance, so that it is the great duty of man, in all the departments of life, to give that spirit fuller and fuller entrance. "Lift up your heads."

Christ is kept out of our lives, not only in our practice, but as a rule of living. The men of this age are not living under even a rule of absolute perfection, — far from it, — but under a rule allowed to be more or less loose and accommodated. The rule set up is not only an adaptation, but a compromise; not only an adaptation to the necessary, but an unnecessary compromise with the world. For example, the considerations of rank in aristocratic communities, while it is right they should modify the rule of Christian brotherhood, do in fact so much compromise and lower the rule towards the mean and poor as to make it not a little unchristian.

But this non-admission of the pure Christian rule is prominently and painfully evident in international and civil law, in business and society. International law has yet to lift the head of its gates much higher for the full entrance of the King of glory; for hitherto and until lately it has been contracted down to self and the rule of mere power. Even civil law, the boast of the reason and justice of men, must yet lift the roof of its temple, if it would let in the full soul of Christ. And as to society and business, they need not be spoken of. The law of the lady and gentleman, the rule of the man of honor and of the woman of fashion, the usage of the merchant, are evidently not illumined by the full presence of the King of glory.

The reminder, then, to-day is to admit a purer Christian usage into all the great departments of life; but specially, let me say, in the great relations of rich and poor, the employer and the laborer. Before us appears an insurrection of labor, amounting almost to a revolution. We ask why? Whatever else may be also true, it is clear that the spirit of Christ is not in our business, — at least not in the workshop side of it, — for it is an insurrection with less cause, less justification, than in any case ever heard of in the history of man. If such are the acts of our people under little, perhaps no oppression, under little suffering, what ought to be the outbreak of the poor English laborer, and what ought the French Revolution to have been, under the cruel, indescribable wrongs of that people? Some self-sacrifice, of course, was necessary to our workmen; but to bear nothing to help the country and brotherhood, groaning as it now is under its many burdens, and at the first touch of wrongs (chiefly imaginary) to break from law and destroy, may show at least how much labor is pampered and spoiled in America. To many despondent people it seems to show more. They see in the wild outbreak along the avenues of commerce in many States, in the long lines of burning property, in mobs commanding that trade shall stop, — in the horror and glare of all this they see the very face of French communism. Yet to tamper with it will, in my judgment, make it a much more serious business; to speak soft words to it, to fraternize with malefactors, — I mean the real malefactors, for I know that the workman was often innocent or half innocent, — I say for the sake of interest or false pity to be recreant to law on the part of the responsible classes, will show that the real spirit of the law of Christ is not only not in the workshop, but not in the parlor of the president and the director, or the homes of stockholders. Of course, give to the worthy workman full justice. If the times are hard, the Christian will give better wages and sweeten them with kindness; but the spirit of Christianity is not weak, is not a silly mercy. It will, to the misguided, give correction, with pity; but to the thieving incendiary, the wanton insurrectionist, it gives the cold hand of law, — it gives reluctant but unflinching force. Shall we let such as you ruin the Ark of God?

I speak in view of great interests injured; but far beyond that, in view of law violated under a free government of the people. And my view is that if the wrong be as great and uncalled for as it seems to be, so great and decided and exemplary should be the settlement. To be settled fitly, it must be settled, if not by an eminence of penalty as great as the crime, yet the settlement should be exemplary; and if settled otherwise, the spirit of good government is deserting both sides of our business. Law, — law is the only king of a free people; to withstand it with violence is next to treason, and is, as the apostle says, "to bring to ourselves damnation." "When I go into a country," Montesquieu once remarked, "I do not inquire whether they have good laws (for these they have everywhere), but I ask whether these laws are executed." If we Americans lose the honor of executed laws, we lose the common honor of Christian civilization.

After great sacrifices this outbreak will of course be mastered, and the country awake from this hideous dream. But the sign and proof will remain of a deep vice in society, the first great sign among us of the reversal of the evils of old society; that is, tyranny and outrage at the top of society beginning to be changed to tyranny and outrage from the bottom. And the question is, Has this vice shown itself too late for remedy? Ah! we stood still and allowed the government of our fathers (itself a perilous but most benign experiment), we stood still and allowed the politician to change it into a new experiment, — the experiment of a government of mere numbers. We gave the vote to ignorance and barbarism from abroad and to ignorance and barbarism at home, and are now surprised that power seems to be passing downwards, and begins to assert itself as *King at the bottom*. It is a call to deep thought. We have allowed to pass from our hands one of our very greatest securities.

Still, I am not one of those who take too gloomy a view of the future, and who think that in the midst of our rich country we are sitting as Belshazzar at the Feast, while the fingers of a man's hand are writing doom upon the wall. I do not feel in this way. We have a main security left, I think. It is not in the rich, it is not in the poor, but in that enormous class of moderate and small capitalists which makes the real body of the American people, whose interests and sympathies are with order, and whose mass is so great that it can never be shaken by outbreak. Were the nation divided into the few rich and the many poor, there would be no security for one hour; but now in any question between labor and capital that great intermediate class, which is in effect a mediating class, must declare for order; for they have come up by acquiring even a little property, they have come up into the class of order. They have undergone the magic process by which the radical becomes a conservative as if in a moment. They have entered upon civilization. There may be sudden outbreaks of the laborers or the idle, but they can never become vital so long as the interests and feelings of this wide middle mass are against them. So that though there may be, and probably will be, gradual but orderly encroachments on the rights of great wealth,— that is much to be feared, for we have some proof of it already,— yet that will not be great while the permanent existence of society and of a government administered in the interests of the body of the people are, I think, sure.

So much I am happy to say. With all our shocks and fears, this I believe to be a government as permanent as any. But to make society something better than this, to make it worthy of the hope with which it began, that is a different thing; for that we have much to do. The spirit of Christ must come in, the heads of the gates, the everlasting doors of the heart, must be lifted, that the King of glory may enter. A nation, I repeat, we shall continue to be,— a nation great in material interests, guarded by the instincts of a thriving people; but nothing beyond this is feasible without patriotism towards the State and a Christian heart in our business and society, and specially a Christian heart in that great relation of the poor and the rich. Education, as it is called, will do something; but character, far more Christ, or at least some shadow of Christ, must enter into all departments, — specially, as I have said, into the workshop and the palace, — and turn the hearts of the fathers to the children, and of the children to the fathers, and in the spirit of grateful love from below, and of generous love from above, bind together the mighty opposites of society.

So far I have spoken as if bearing more against the poor than the rich; but I have done so simply because here and at the present moment it seems to be just, for power here sways to the side of the poor (after long centuries of injustice and sorrow), and I rejoice at it; and only because it begins to be abused do I denounce the abuse. I speak in the interests not merely of the rich but of the poor man, whom I would save from himself to keep our noble Christian law for his children. Were this England, I hope I should be ashamed to do as the English Established pulpit did, or many of its clergy, for three centuries, and nearly until to-day. I should be ashamed to stand up on the side of place and power, flattering them, and treading into lower submission the brotherhood already so far down. But here and now the case is much changed. England is growing gloriously right, and we, in the other direction, are growing wrong.

I have said enough on the one side, and must turn

before I close for a moment to the other, and exhort the rich to let the beautiful spirit of the King of glory appear in them more and more. And whom do I mean by the rich? I mean not four or five of eminent wealth, — I mean almost all the people before me, nay, those much below the class before me. And I say to all, Let Christ appear in us. There is much demand for his presence, I assure you. You will not find your duty easy; for the temper of the poor and rich is, if not naturally opposed, easily made so, hide the fact as we may. The interests of labor and capital look to be different. And so the proud rich and the proud poor make a dreadful jar together. Christ's gracious sweetness is the only secret of cure on the part of the rich, and yet it is very hard for them to acquire and keep it. It is easy to be sentimental about brotherhood, to talk about it in church, but hard facts try it. For the poor and our dependents often require of us as much forbearance as children, without the interest of children; and that we should in the face of all our distastes "consider" the poor, — his bad birth, his bad education, which have shaped his soul badly, — "consider him and forbear him," that is not easy. For the self-sacrifice of the rich is hard while it is so pleasant and easy to use power indolently and contemptuously. Even with a little of Christ's spirit, there is still no such beautiful brotherhood as might easily be made between poor and rich. Even in this country, where many of the poor are half spoiled, and many of the rich half spoiled, still the heart of the poor man is easily touched by the consideration of the rich man, and the rich man's heart responds quickly to right feeling in the poor. Ah! if but the shadow of Christ's kindness were to fall into either class, it would make life beautiful. Hear then, my high brother, my high sister, and suffer this word of exhortation: "Masters, give unto your servants that which is just and equal, remembering that you also have a master in heaven." Are you already liberal of your gifts and kindness for the good of the poor and for the public good? God be praised! And is your kindness well considered and wise and graciously given? God be praised! And is there no blame for lack of sympathy, for proud and unfeeling distance from "the brotherhood of low degree"? Then God be praised! And do you persist in your goodness though ingratitude and mean criticism surround you? Then God be most praised! Well done! Your heart remembers him. You have fulfilled the sweet charge of the divine apostle: "Charge them that are rich in this world, that they be not high-minded, nor trust in uncertain riches, but in the living God; . . . that they do good, that they be rich in good works, ready to distribute, willing to communicate, laying up in store for themselves treasures in heaven; . . . who being rich, yet for our sakes became poor, that we through his poverty might be made rich."

XXVIII.

THEY REWARDED EVIL FOR GOOD.

They rewarded me evil for good, to the spoiling of my soul. —
Ps. xxxv. 12.

MAN is made by society; yet unmade also. In ways suspected and unsuspected each man is really injured as well as benefited by his fellows; and it would be an art indeed, — that of getting the good, and guarding from the evil of society. The amount of this evil is great, and the forms of it are various. Take the case of slighted genius, — " the vision and the faculty divine," — which goes through a whole generation without a smile, while all the rewards of the world are poured into the lap of word-mongers: that surely makes the heart ache. While men of genius are left in garrets, we see the thrones of society occupied with men whose places are in the garrets! And when, added to this, superior gifts are accompanied with painful labors and preparations, and when they are blended with high characteristics of soul, as in many sorts of ability they necessarily are, then of course the injustice becomes great, of treating them with a blindness that will not discriminate, or with indifference or neglect.

"They rewarded me evil for good, to the spoiling of my soul." The thing especially meant by good here is, first, where a man has done or is trying to do his duty in general; that sort of good when he is conscious that he has done no wrong, or conscious only of simple-hearted good wishes. The young are the most obvious example of this. Most young people of the better sort begin life honestly and with fine wishes and enthusiasms. Starting thus with high instincts, abhorring meanness, and expecting from men what they feel in themselves, blow after blow of injustice strikes them; they are awakened into a horrible reality; dashed, outraged, and embittered; then they recover, and are again thrown off and recover, and recover until the recovering power is gone; or if not so bad as that, if the tenacity of their hearts towards good remains, still the inward spring is much broken, they expect little and will do little, and their justification or excuse for the remnant of their days is spoken sadly, or spoken bitterly: "They rewarded me evil for good, to the spoiling of my soul."

> "Candid and generous and just,
> Boys care but little whom they trust, —
>   An error soon corrected:
> For who but learns in riper years
> That man when smothered he appears
>   Is most to be suspected?"

But the same injury occurs all through a man's life, and it is partly an importunate necessity of our state that we should so be treated. Our life and conduct are always open to misconstruction because of the natural ignorance we have of one another, or because of the weak judgment of many people, or because many are either of poor hearts originally, or they themselves have been spoiled by the same sort of bad treatment long ago, and so are suspicious, and look at everything on the worst side. Here, then, each man is surrounded by a multitude of such judges, a cloud of such witnesses, most of them unauthorized, either by natural fitness, to judge, or uncalled to it by their connection with the thing in hand, "busybodies in other men's matters," or at least incapable, by their real ignorance of the matter, to bear any testimony or to give any judgment; yet almost all, and usually in proportion to their unfitness, are quick to give decisions or piercing suggestions about the vital concerns of others! As to which I say in passing, that if contempt could speak down from heaven to this host of officious usurpers of judgment, its speech would be, "Who made you a ruler or a judge?"

Here then, either from the natural weakness or the common pettiness of men, there is a sort of necessity for much ill treatment. "It must needs be that offences come." But when to all these natural or at least usual incapacities of treating one another nobly is added the simple fact that your look, demeanor, ways, are not shaped to all men's fancies, or much more, when there is added some personal feeling, — a hurt vanity, an envy, a spiteful grudge, a keen instinct against another which is awake to watch him, — then of course the ill treatment will (if it dare) go much farther; and how far it then can go, how utterly men can sink even the recollection of justice, almost every one has occasion at some time to learn. The Psalms of David are full of notices of such conduct among those enemies of his; and we, though so much more civilized here, have much of the same thing under smooth pretence and quiet unwarlike manners.

Whether from the common weakness of men, or from personal prejudices or spite, the offence will come. And it is almost as certain that every time it does come, every time the innocent man meets such treatment, it takes off some of his brotherly kindness or hopefulness, and turns some more drops of the sweet milk in his bosom into gall. Every man's personal experience will give him enough instances of this. We can all remember, I suppose, where at some personal sacrifice we intended some worthy thing and were met with unthankfulness, perhaps with even an ingenuity of misconstruction and a wantonness of wrong. We remember how it touched and shrunk our hearts, and after years have passed, and when we can look back without the least personal feeling, but only in solemn and melancholy review, we murmur to ourselves, "They did me evil and it injured me." It is true, in this judgment we may rate our own cause too favorably, as self usually does; still there are many times when our view of the case is either altogether or mainly just. The outraged Lear in that great poem which I cannot name without seeing its sceptred pall come sweeping through my imagination, in that poem which in the grandeur of its tragic element seems written by the sublimest genius of sorrow, — there, the old king, rent and blasted, no doubt because of his proud precipitancy, was himself the starting cause of his own woes! Yet he was but just to himself when he said, —

> "I am a man
> More sinned against than sinning."

Though he were not clear, yet he was wronged, spoiled, maddened! Could I open the long roll of cases only less tragical, the long roll of man's foolish or malignant wrongs to man; could we but catch a glimpse of the thing as it is now, through empires, cities, streets, and most of all in families; could all the varieties and shades and singularities of this injustice be painted to our eyes; and could we but see how this wrong worked out on all sides grief and wretchedness and every shape of pain, how the better sort of human beings, and often the sweetest and best, were heart-wrung by a harder and baser class below them, — ah! could we look deeper into the spirits of men, and see the spiritual poison of injustice; if we could see how the sweet turned at its cursed touch to bitter, faith to distrust, how the generous expansions of the heart were contracted and shrivelled all through, as a cold storm shrivels and blasts the tender germ in the spring; if we could watch the spirit of wrong moving like a night through society, or as a secret pestilence through the great atmosphere of the globe! Appalling, I say. No talk of it can match it. We are not aware of the black influence poured out by our thoughtless injustice. Take heed! "Take heed that ye offend not one of these little ones." What does the Lord mean? He means, I think, in its broadest sense to guard the defenceless, the comparatively harmless people from the strong and comparatively unscrupulous, not merely to defend the weak. He means in his mercy to erect a defence for the spirit of man against man. And he adds, — and there are but few things like it among his words, — "It were better for that man that a millstone were hung about his neck and that he were drowned in the depths of the sea." Let us take heed. If we do not follow the sacrifices of Christ, who always gave himself for others, yet at least we can be of the spirit which hates the baseness of injustice, cannot bear to spoil another's heart, and will be just, and purely just, at any cost! We can rise to that at least. If I cannot be a Christian, I must at least be as noble as a Roman or a Greek. If it were not that there is a sun that daily rises on this night and purges it; if it were not that there is another spirit descended from heaven and moving on the face of society, which by gracious influences corrects and sweetens, — if it were not for this, justice could not stem the tide, man would destroy man, and all souls perish: which brings me to the second topic, the way the Christian soul is to meet all this evil.

"But I say unto you, love your enemies." Let wrong not arouse more wrong; but if hell itself invades you, let that but prompt your soul to break out like a new heaven to meet it. There are people who will take one evil and make ten out of it. They are like a broken mirror, and reflect and give back every image of evil from a thousand distorted bits and in a thousand distorted aspects. But we must thank God that there are other people who check the tide of wrong, convert it, and transfigure it into good,— people who if it rained curses would turn them into blessings at the moment they touched the ground. "But I say unto you, love ye your enemies." If you do but do good to them who do good to you again, do not even the publicans so? Do not even the wretches so? But the children of your Father have a far better style, "for he sendeth his rain upon the just and unjust." The evil of the earth does not spoil the sweet heavens and make them like iron and shut up their rains; and shall it spoil you, a child of the heavens? Remember the spirit you are of. The earth has been full of the heroes of hate, but it arrives at last to the heroes of love. There is not an apostle, not a disciple on the pages of the New Testament who is not majestic in mercy. The keener, more vivid, more vengeful and wilful the man, the finer he is touched and made over to a heavenly sort of endurance and pity. See Peter, the impetuous. Recompense to no man "evil for evil, or railing for railing: but contrariwise, blessing." See Paul. "Even unto this present hour we both hunger, and thirst, and are naked, and are buffeted, and have no certain dwelling-place; . . . being reviled we bless; being persecuted we suffer it: being defamed we entreat." And oh, above all, remember Christ's majesty of righteousness and love, what sort and quality that was; that though they rewarded him evil for good, — such evil for such good, — it was not to the spoiling of his soul. " He was not overcome of the evil, but overcame evil with good; " and at the very moment when wrong had reached the top, and the cup was full, and he wrung out its bitterness, he said, " Father, forgive them: for they know not what they do." They did know what they did, the heavens themselves charged them when it was night over the whole land from the sixth to the ninth hour; but his divinely generous construction even at that moment hoped and believed that at the centre they were ignorant, and shielded them from the wrath of justice, and said, " Father, forgive them: for they know not what they do."

XXIX.

THE POWER OF WILL.

Whosoever will, let him take the water of life freely. — REV. xxii. 17.
All things are possible to him that believeth. — MARK, ix. 23.

I SPEAK first of the power of human will in our life, especially in religious life. It seems to me that the idea of soul-freedom — of a power of choice in ourselves — is a practical necessity; for a man cannot be human, or lead a human life, without consciousness of free-will. If this is granted, and the full weight given to it, if we start with the consciousness of such a spirit in ourselves, then all the other great mysteries outside of ourselves which puzzle us so much — the mystery of God, of God acting in miracle, the efficacy of prayer — are intelligible; but without this we must give up all religion, all idea of spirit, shut our Bibles and Moral Codes, — understanding all such things in a non-natural sense, — go on to reduce the world and God and man to a few simple and eternal brute forces. For if we ourselves are things, not wills, then we can know of nothing spiritual except from ourselves; all else must be things also. As God and spirit and spiritual acts are all taken from the image of ourselves, then, if we are things, we can know nothing but things.

The whole outside spiritual world rests on the sureness of our consciousness of a spirit in ourselves, — the possession of a will. I mention this merely to show how sure the fact is that we have wills, — for God and a spiritual universe all rest upon that fact, — and I mention it also to give a basis to the exhortation I wish to make; for if we have such a wonderful power, we should believe in it, and use it to its full extent.

There is this singularity in this matter; namely, that though our natures are made free, yet if we do not believe that and use their freedom, if we believe we are the creatures of circumstances, we become the creatures of circumstances, and, as much as we can, we become things; while a full assurance that we can do much, that we are made for a wide sweep of power, gives us the full freedom we were born to. It will not do that we are made free; we must also believe the fact before we can be free practically.

Of course there is a limit to the power of will, and only the insane will attempt to go beyond obvious natural bounds. But while we must know that, let us beware of contracting these bounds too closely around us; while we are in fact eagles, made to sweep the great circles of the air, let us not confine ourselves, like the moth or the butterfly, to a few feet of the fields. No man can certainly say where his power stops; or, if he knows where it stopped yesterday, he does not know how far it will go to-morrow. It is a growing power, which ascends as we use it. In the ordinary concerns of life we exert this power very much, though there are great differences in this respect among men and ages. The will as used in the bettering of our material state, that is, determined enterprise, is a majestic power here in America, and a mere petty power in Spain, and still more petty in the East, and sinks down to its weakest among the low savages.

But nowhere is the religious will used as it ought to be. To be determined in religion, to be industrious Christians, seem strange expressions. Yet to be determined Christians is just what we want,—to set the will "like flint" against wrong; to make "full proof" of all the religious capacities of our souls; to be bent to exercise all Christian virtues as we exercise our muscles or our business energies; to make an advance every day, as any true worker advances in his knowledge, or in his fortune, and says in the evening, "I have gained so much, I have mastered so much."

Was there ever in business or war an intenser expression of spiritual energy than when Paul said, "This one thing I do"? He used the whole scope of his will. His poor hard-worked body solicited him for some ease, for some rest, for a little comfort. His poor human heart sunk under discouragements, shrunk from calumny, quailed under fears. Did he pause?

"This one thing I do." He saw iniquity in the church, littleness in its leaders, — poor, scattered results, — an opposing world growing greater and more impregnable before him; did he halt? "This one thing I do."

A thousand things sapped his faith; for one example, Christ did not come from the skies as he expected, and that great test of the truth of all his soul rested on failed him. Did he sink? Nay, his faith enlarged; he was surer of God and surer of Christ when his expectations failed than even when they were realized. Let everything fail, I will believe; and I will believe in a mightier and mightier fashion, for when this and that give way I will fall back on the strength of the dictates of my soul. "Though flesh and heart fail," I will grow a purer, more disinterested, more believing, more powerful servant of God. I will do it to the end. And he did it, — glory and honor to him!

Myriads of creatures are born with this divine will-power. Of course I do not say in the same degree as Paul, but with the same faculty; and they die like great embryonic masses, undeveloped souls, which have never come to anything. Here and there is one man who lives and proves that he is a being with a divine will, — proves it, too, all the more powerfully, when circumstances are all against him.

These awful things, — circumstances, — whose power is the talk of this age, which are so weighty that they forbid religion and laugh at morality, — these overpowering circumstances, which shrivel us up as before a fire, which will not allow us to have a soul within our bosoms, and which we set up openly with shameless faces as our excuse before man, yes, and before God. "Circumstances are against us." And what are these circumstances? They are but a shadow wherever there is present a greater circumstance; namely, the pure, unconquerable will, which overrides them, which converts them, the worst of them, and makes its diamonds out of all such charcoal. You are a will, I say, and hence you are, by the very intention of your nature, made to dominate, made for triumph over circumstance.

We are ever losing our humanity, because to be human means to be under the control of righteous will. We are the prey of almost everything without us, and of almost every vagrant passion within us. We are made to govern ourselves by the righteous law, — not self-degraded mortals, but pure, immortal wills. I speak this, not for the purpose of pride, but that we may be instigated to reject every day the whole world of flesh and self, and to accept whatever is humble, generous, and just, pure, and adoring, — to do this in our thoughts and in our work, being as God-made men in all the details of our living. It is a large and awful work; all the more must we push it while the day lasts. "I will arise," must be the motto of every moment.

When I think of men, hundreds, almost thousands of millions, appearing and disappearing every thirty years, what a common, cheap creature man is! But when I think that each of these men has a *will*, — is made to enact into existence all righteousness, — that he is formed to work together with God in the awful, universal conflict between good and evil, then I stand back before the meanest man, for he makes the very earth sacred. Oh that some power, some voice would speak to him and make this grand possibility real. But our wishes are worthless if a man does not help himself.

There are two sources of power in a man, — the God-given will is one, the God-given trust is another. The mere will is cold and cheerless without the trust, and the trust is weak and boneless without the will. Man must add to the power of his own spirit the power of the spirit of God. It is comparatively easy to be a man of will only; it is comparatively easy to have only the woman's pre-eminent faith and trust: but the duty is to have both working together in our ordinary lives; to cast ourselves, like the most helpless children, upon the parent's breast, — to receive of his fulness, and "to quit us like men" in the daily strife of temptation and effort. If we do all well that is within our will, heavenly glimpses open, lights and powers stream in, and the spontaneous life of the soul grows. Then "be it unto thee even as thou wilt" must have this other sentence added, "All things are possible to him that trusteth." Rest on your soul as if there were no other power in heaven or earth; but your soul must rest on God as if there were no such thing known as will, and "the gates of hell shall not prevail against you."

XXX.

THE WISDOM OF GOD.

To the intent that now unto the principalities and powers in heavenly places might be known by the church the manifold wisdom of God. — EPH. iii. 10.

THE apostle, having been speaking of the mysterious but wise method of Divine Providence in the rejection of the Jews and acceptance of the Gentiles, now states that this and of course all similar instances are intended to instruct other portions of his universe. I say, this and of course all similar instances; for if so small a thing as this mystery was, comparatively, was intended to spread aloft to the high angels of God, we cannot think that the deeper and more significant facts are to be kept private here to man.

This diffusion of moral knowledge from the earth through the heavens is often stated by Christians as a probable thing; but I am surprised that that which is here made clear and certain should be spoken of at all as probable. There could be no expression of a truth more explicit. Apart from this direct assurance, however, the same thing might have been supposed, had we never been told it, from what we see in Nature.

God everywhere in Nature is economical of his means, and has everywhere established such connections between his works that every portion may be and is used in some way for the benefit of some or all other. Indeed, in the whole of creation, so far as we know, there is not one atom made independent, or put out of sympathy — if I may so speak — with the mass. Every part of our earth, for example, is united with every other part. There is a constant interchange of physical influences through every part of it.

It is so also with its social and moral influences. There can be no eminent example of good or evil in the condition of one nation that is not influential all round the globe directly or indirectly. So far at least as this region of God's works is concerned, he has designed a close society, and works out his mightiest effects through the power of one part on another. This great principle operates not merely between what is contemporaneous, but also between the past and the future.

As objects and men the most distant in place may operate on each other to-day, so as to what is most distant in time. The action and events of all past history concentrate their influence in the present. This is undeniable. It is also undeniable that, so far as advance or improvement is made, there is a tendency to perfect the social character of this system. The parts of the earth's surface are brought nearer together; the interchange of interest and influence between all races and tribes becomes fuller and more effective. So, also, as nations advance, the power of the present over the future becomes greater of course. Just in proportion as a tribe of men are sunk in barbarism are they bereft of a history, of a past, and its power; and just as a people advance in all that is heroic and excellent in one era, that people become powerful over another.

The clear tendency, then, as men advance, is to perfect the great design of God in constituting them social, to complete the family idea which God had in view, to bind together most closely every part of the race through all time, in all places. This, I say, seems the undeniable design, so far as this earth is concerned.

But does this design extend any farther? Is not this globe and every globe — however clearly a social design is shown within it — cut off from any such relations without it? Does not the very fact that worlds are scattered at such immense distances through space evince not a social but a dissocial purpose? I confess that at first it looks so. But if it is so, it is strange, for God usually maintains a wonderful analogy, or likeness, between all his works. Everything he does, while it is different, is the same. He never repeats himself, and yet is never unlike himself. And as the social principle seems to be one of the very deepest and most cherished of the divine ideas, — if I may so express it, — would it not be wonderful that it should be so completely deserted and given up?

The probabilities then are evidently against that opinion. The probabilities then are strong, I think, even if we were confined in facts to this globe, — even if we had no instances of union between this globe and other worlds. But in fact we have some grand particulars which assure us that the social idea is not deserted, but runs between world and world. No star has ever been discovered, not even the wildest of the comets, which moved alone. The worlds are all made up into splendid groups or families, each influencing each, acting in its measure on every point, even from this low point to the farthest bounds of flaming space. The whole incomprehensible, sublime pageant of the heavens moves and acts together.

It is certain, it is known, that as respects material forces the whole universe interacts; nay, the mightiest of all material forces (perhaps the one which includes all others) is employed and spent in interaction. Now, if this be so with material forces, is it probable that moral forces, influences, of which the powers of matter are but as the shadows and symbols, — moral forces, which we see so constantly and wonderfully at work between man and man, and nation and nation, and age and age, should be confined and ironed in to this earth?

I suppose, of course, you observe that there are other races of spirits, not necessarily inhabitants of these visible worlds, though of that the probabilities are resistless to my mind; but whether embodied in these shining mansions or as purer spirits, other races of spirits the Bible everywhere assumes or states. As to these, then, can we think the great law of the family, which in lower nature we see penetrates everywhere and controls everything, — that this in the higher nature, among the spiritual tribes, is hemmed in to each, and no race and no moral history of one globe ever allowed to act on another? I know not how it may strike your minds, but to me to state it seems enough. Is the grandeur of God's spiritual house to stand so dwindled by the side of his material house? Or, if the theory of the spiritual universe allows it to be progressive (and who now denies that?), what progression, except one comparatively mean, can be effected, according to God's ordinary way of working, but by the wide interaction of various beings and various experiences, each different in character and history, but each alike, and each reflecting some new and startling depth of the central truths of God?

As it is justly supposed that the tribes of men lower in the scale are always lifted — if lifted at all — from without, that the higher life or higher ideas possessed by one part of the family are held in stewardship for others, so I suppose that not only races inferior to man, but orders of creatures higher by nature though less deeply experienced than man, shall receive from his history lifting conceptions, such a new element of angelic civilization as shall transform the whole. Now, how grandly intoned with this comes in the decided and sublime statement of Paul, — "To the intent that now unto the principalities and powers in heavenly places might be known by the church the manifold wisdom of God"! "To the intent;" as if God's schemes here had not only some bearings beyond, but had their chief reference away high up there among the "principalities and powers." If this be true, I regard it as a very great truth indeed.

See, first, the light it casts upon that moral scheme of the world of which Christianity is the development and consummation. In view of the extensiveness of the creation and the littleness of man, there is, at least to many of us, an unfit look in the importance the Bible gives to man in that wonderful story of the descent of the Son of God for the redemption of man through his life and death. Of old there was a mighty feeling of wonder that God in his daily providence should seem so intent on man. "When I consider thy heavens, the work of thy fingers, the moon and the stars which thou hast ordained, what is man that thou art mindful of him?"

But the later events of the gospel — if this feeling were just at all — ought to carry it to a blank amazement. But all is nobly explained when we learn that this earth is made but as a stage around which all the creatures of the heavens, whatever they be, may gather as spectators of the exhibition of God made there, — gather around it now, and when this material earth and heavens have passed away, the history it leaves shall take its place in the very centre of heavenly interest, — the divinest leaf in the history of God and the creature. "And the temple of God was opened in heaven, and there was seen in his temple the ark of his testament: and there were lightnings, and voices, and thunderings, and an earthquake, and great hail."

Again: if this history of God on earth has a universal instructiveness in it as a lesson of races, spreading through all spaces, we must believe that its stretch in time is of equal largeness. If God slowly works out his mysteries through long dispensations, even when they concern but the private affairs of one race and one earth, what times ought we to expect him to employ when he is working out the moral history in which Christ appears, — where the deepest dark and the highest light are revealed together; where the history and nature of good and evil, of God and the creature, is unclosing for the behoof of all places and times? Whenever, then, I see something of awful darkness before which I must bow down, I remember the eternity of God, and the wide, long sweep of his work; I remember that a thousand years in his sight are but as yesterday; seeing that is past as a watch in the night.

But not only do the width and length of the moral scheme of the world lighten its mysteries, there is given also in that a particular dignity to the truth in Christ.

The apostle calls it "the manifold wisdom of God;" the many-folded — the all-various — the wisdom which is the *plena* or *pleroma*, the fulness of all aspects of the divine. This is that divine system, so neglected, which shallow, vain man so often glances at only to despise. But it is not Paul's eulogy of the truth which so much describes its grandeur, as the fact he speaks of, that this manifold wisdom was of so wide significance that it was to be diffused up, even to the "principalities and powers" for their learning.

I cannot say, it is not necessary to say, how all the truths of our Christianity may be useful everywhere; but I think it might be shown that there could be no conceivable height of finite spirits to whom most of its truths would not be new and impressive. For example: that one lesson of God first seen in weakness; what a new conception of God! — a conception not only valuable to correct our ideal of the truly great, but most needed, I may venture to think, to guard the ideal of those resplendent creatures who though innocent are exposed, without some such revelation, — exposed, if to anything, to false ideas of elevation. For how could they in the deepest manner be taught the truest style of divinity, so long as they knew the highest only as the "blessed and only potentate;" so long as the sight of the highest humbling itself to suffering and emptying itself out of love, — so long as that sight, which I suppose to reveal the deepest deep of God, was kept back from them?

But, just glancing at the dignity which this fact gives to truth, I must go on, that I may pause a moment upon the dignity it gives to man and all that concerns him. This his home is now no distant and all but forgotten spot, but a central region, it seems, a chosen spot of revelation. Man perishing before the moth is an actor where God and angels are the spectators, and is working out every day not merely his own imperishable lot, but is working out matter for the instruction, for the cheer or the sorrow, of regions where other suns shine, and of ages which shall come on after our ages have passed. Under this body, under this form of heart and mind which belongs to me, the inexpressible Word of God did its inexpressible work; so that there shall go with us — whether we sink or rise — perhaps an altogether peculiar interest, unknown to the highest creatures, gathered from our mysterious fellowship with the only-begotten of God.

"Upon these creatures," will they say, — "upon them, by them, and through them was made an exhibition of the divine nature, which, as by a new illumination, has relit every scene of creation and the vision of every spirit. Lo! this is man!"

So associated then with the Lamb of God, carrying in our commonest acts and days such a weight of results, —

> "So, and not searching higher, we may learn
> To prize the breath we share with humankind,
> And look even upon the dust of man with awe."

We may learn, being "compassed about with so great a cloud of witnesses," to awake to our calling: in trial to run with patience the wonderful race that is set before us, to fill our hearts with these high incitements, each man living as if upon him, even such an one, all the holy and wise faces were turned; as if upon him lay the illustration of all God's scheme, of all Christ's love, — as if upon him. Did I say "as if"? Upon him it is laid, that now "unto the principalities might be known" by him, here, to-day, under these ordinary risings and settings of the sun, here, under these familiar, homely names, places, and acts, — by him might be known, by his Christ-likeness, by his showing in himself the whole fruits and glory of the Redeemer and the redemption, — might be known by him, in the few days which run before they carry his body to the dust, — might be made known by him new secrets, even to the "principalities and powers," — new secrets of the great deep of the manifold wisdom of God.

XXXI.

THE RIVER OF LIFE.

There is a river the streams whereof shall make glad the city of God. — Ps. xlvi. 4.

THE greatest possible gift to the world would be the gift of a nobler and better soul in the bosom of each man. That soul includes everything. For the civilized soul would make of course the civilized society, the civilized government: the quickened and elevated heart alone can put all the faculties of man, all arts, all works, into the highest action, with the highest aims, and turn man's consciousness, his life, his society, his earth, from a weak, impure, and unhappy state, into a state where there is power for feebleness, purity for corruption, peace for disturbance, and so convert earth into the highest conception of heaven. All out of the heart! As the heart is, everything is: if the heart be a thistle-seed, its whole world will be a sproutage of thistle; if it be "wholly a right seed," it will spring up into a world of fruit. Our need then is more soul, more light and life of the heart.

What an announcement then is the text, "There is a river the streams whereof shall make glad the city of

God." There is a descending flood of renovation! There is a spirit! If the wishes of the heart could create a belief, it would be bliss, for this is at once the most rational, poetical, pure, and desirable belief possible to man. So we find that wherever man is pure and high, an era of descending spirit is always looked forward to. The Lord himself about to leave the earth in darkness and after a life which seemed a failure, — shall I say? — announced the coming and the reign of spirit on earth. And to make the fact sensible to the eye and ear, as Christians believe, see, hear, the rushing of a mighty wind, "the house shaken where they were sitting," the tongues like as of fire, the little congregation rushing forth and bursting into a various language, each man of the assembled strangers speaking in his own speech the wonderful works of God. See and hear the joy, the excitement, the men almost abandoned and reckless in a divine delirium; if not "drunk with new wine," filled indeed with a new and better wine from the grapes of God!

That something mighty had taken place was attested, how? By new souls; by the fact that something had made the Christians into powers. Read the letters of Peter and Paul, and you will see that a new race, gigantic, incredible, has been on the earth. And then, their joy. We view the early Christians all on one side, as sufferers. But on the other side, there never was such a period of joy. The footsteps of Astræa seemed to be returning to the world, heaven coming back to earth. "I will send the Comforter unto you;" and he was indeed sent. Was ever a promise so rapidly and amply fulfilled? Their joy was full. They had "with persecutions" a hundred-fold of everything good. They reaped the two great beatitudes: meek, they possessed the earth; pure in heart, they saw God!

Christians believe all this. It is their belief also that this but introduced an era of spirit. That first great moment is gone like a splendid dream. But it is not to be regarded as an anomaly, appearing once, like the sense of beauty in Greece, and to reappear no more. It has prepared the way for new wonders. It has pushed far forward the possibilities of man, has erected standards which will never be taken down, and has left in the world a church, dwelling to be sure in a long twilight of spirit, but awaiting another burst of day. Such is God's way. His truth advances by bursts of splendor, and then by long ages in which the light is worked into the general life.

But whatever wonders await us, one thing we know: The spirit never will, never does reappear, unless it is waited for, and asked for by some pure spiritual faith in us. There is one sure law, that only "to him that hath shall be given." God waits for man to feel need. A certain degree of the very gift looked for must first exist. When man rises a suppliant towards the heavens, the heavens will descend towards him, and not until then.

Now, as to this need and faith the future seems dark.

In addition to the usual faithlessness of the worldly soul, has come in the growing belief in matter not in spirit, in law and not in a person; so that faith which I should define to be trust in the moral soul of the universe, that is, a person, that is, God, — this seems dying out of the soul. But there is hope. I believe, though I cannot now explain, that the empire of natural law which science is now unfolding is the precursor, the condition, the instigation, and the mould, of such an appearance of spirit, of such an empire of God, as has never been dreamed of. But this we who are now alive will not see. That vast Pentecost is reserved until after a long process is through, when that which hinders shall be taken out of the way. Meanwhile each of us, for himself, can, at least in a measure, free himself from the material and worldly spirit of the age and of his own heart; each one may live with God, and walk with him, and be surrounded by all the powers of the world to come.

This subject is suggested by the breaking forth of the spring, when Nature stands up created once more, and the spirit is presented so near to us. I would like to see the feast of Whitsunday placed on one of the first and most magnificent days of the spring, when every eye can see the same spirit at work in Nature on the grandest scale. Or, next to that, I would place it after some great summer drought, when the heavens are opened and the rains descend and the change in Nature is such as in one of the Pampas after a South American rain, — odors, grasses, flowers, and gay insects, new life in the eye of man, and freshness and joy among the herds of the field. After a great drought or winter Nature is a picture unrolled from the east to the west, symbolizing all the renewal of God, symbolizing the renewal of human body and spirit yet to come, and especially symbolizing that final spring, when " Behold, I create all things new," shall be pronounced, and all the creation of God shall say, " Amen, even so, Lord God Almighty; " and the old creation with all its shapes of sin and grief shall pass away, and "be no more remembered, nor come again into mind."

Let us pause a moment before this scene of spirit! Surely God is in the earth, though we know it not. But some may say it is only motion, heat, light, or subtler forces, poured through the infinite moulds of the world, — that is all. Away with such words. What and whence these beneficent agents we call motion, heat, and light; whence these infinite moulds of wisdom and love and beauty; whence the transmutation of motion and heat up into conscious life? Wake up and see this great sight of the presence of God. Walk around, mark, adore. The awful Beneficence is at work. In the presence of the Everlasting God from whom I come, to whom I go, be still, my selfish heart; be still, my selfish cares; turn, my poor conceited soul, all into reverence and worship. In this presence I feel my impurity; I confess and cleanse myself from iniquity A mercy like the mercy of Christ seems spread all through Nature, a redeeming tenderness. I remember the gospel pity and the gospel hopes with new assurance, and I believe that God will forgive us our sins, and as he has brought Nature from winter, will bring us up also, and all those who sleep in him!

> " Sin-blighted though we are,
> We too, the reasoning sons of men,
> From our oblivion, winter, called
> Shall rise, and breathe again;
> And in eternal summer lose
> Our threescore years and ten."

The spirit in Nature at this moment is not only a picture of the final conquests of spirit, but of that joyful conquest which is found in the life of every good man, even in his homely days now and here. The usual history of the spirit in the heart is a history of struggle; the spirit is usually with us in the form of the angel with whom Jacob wrestled at midnight. God does not work as we would; but if a man is faithful to his light, he will make a spring out of the cold and dark days of the winter, and he will come into a time of conquest and peace.

And if we really understand the matter, we would make this conquest and peace and springtime perpetual. But we must make a reality of the spirit. To many, the doctrine of the spirit seems a foreign and unnatural thing, a fanatical doctrine. Why should we not be interested in our God? In the beautiful mythology of the Greeks, their gods peeped out from behind the trees, from the floods, and glimpses of them were seen on the hill-tops, and life was full of gods; and where they were not present themselves, they crowded their cities with images of them; and lest any should be omitted, they erected in one place an altar to the unknown God! They loved and delighted in their poor gods. We have a God, we have a spirit, yet many of us are ashamed of the unspeakable dignity of knowing him, — of walking in his presence with awe and love and confession. That spirit has made and fashioned me, and not made me a beast but a man, and through it I live; it is in me and around me in benefits and mercies, and it promises forgiveness and life and higher power when I sink into the grave; it is over all. Shall we not rejoice in it, and open our arms wide to it, and live in it and walk in it? "There is a river the streams whereof shall make glad the city of God."

XXXII.

WORLDLINESS.

They are of the world. — 1 JOHN iv. 5.

THIS is said, not contemptuously, but despairingly. Your natural impression will be that I am to speak against the world; but that is not the case. I cannot speak against the Creator or his world; I cannot speak against any part of the nature he has given us, even if it has been injured by sin or criminal excess. It is not wrong, but right, that a man should be what he was born to be, — a creature of this world, fully living in it, making much of it. The time was when the world was thought, and it is now thought by many, a horrible place, to which the spirit was banished for the sake of whipping it into virtue, — a magical garden whose beauties we must not enjoy because the Devil is behind them, and into which we are brought that we may say No to everything it contains.

But we are learning lately that the world is a great, God-given establishment, not to pass away in a moment by any means, full of God's riches; and that to improve it, to weed out of society and Nature everything which is against man, to make this a place sound and healthy to the bodies and souls of all its children, even the poorest, for generations to come, to be a man of this world, with these views, living in it intelligently, beneficently, enjoyingly, — this we must not call worldly, but rather heavenly. The unworldly, ghastly man who denies all this is spurious, not a real man, — a singular growth of the Middle Ages, his very pictures hateful to the eye; and if we had not pity and even reverence for the mistaken, sincere, and often noble soul, we would shut the door upon him, burying him and his history in the grave where he belongs.

But let me come into some detail of this thought. First, I do not call worldly a love of the beautiful in any of its forms. A sense of the beautiful, a desire for the creation of it, is a part of our " image of God," our soul's likeness to him who " made everything beautiful in his time." Poetry is not a *vinum dæmonum;* painting and sculpture and architecture are not idolatries. These are not worldly. Nor do I call beautiful houses, furniture, equipage, worldly, where they are not the expression of mere vulgar ambition and vulgar waste. Where they modestly correspond to the situation, they are the fit surroundings of a being who, though he has sinned, is still a natural prince at the head of a beautiful and princely creation, to whom a monkish squalor is a disgrace and indeed a sort of spiritual insanity.

Nor is taste, even when spent in adorning the person in beautiful dress, unworthy. The young maiden adorns herself instinctively; and when this is done with modesty and moderation, who shall tell her Nay? You will remind me of Saint Peter: " Whose adorning let it not be that outward adorning of plaiting the hair, and of wearing of gold, or of putting on of apparel; but let it be . . . that which is not corruptible, even the ornament of a meek and quiet spirit, which is in the sight of God of great price. For after this manner in the old time the holy women also, who trusted in God, adorned themselves."

But he speaks of "holy women," while I am speaking of all people. Moreover, the spirit of this passage is, "Whose adorning let it not be so much that outward as this inward adorning," just as any sober person would now-say, where he saw an excessive vanity of ornament. Such a passage, taken strictly, is one of asceticism, and would reduce men in their habits to monks, and every woman to a nun, and is not at all in accordance with the spirit of Him who came eating and drinking, and who said, "Consider the lilies how they grow: they toil not, they spin not; and yet I say unto you, that Solomon in all his glory was not arrayed like one of these." He who with his own hands painted the wings and crest of the bird, who curves and sculptures every wave cast upon the shore; he who made the beautiful human form and that most exquisite work, a human countenance; he who can do nothing that is ugly, any more than he can do anything that is foolish, — shall we slander him by deforming and disgracing the body, the high temple of the Spirit?

But when the splendors of my house or my dress are the ends of my being; when I devote work and money and thought to the coverings of a perishing body, and do nothing for the imperishable heart; when everything is done for the eye of man, and nothing for the eye of God, — nay, when every beauty and ornament, through my vanity or envy, discolors and makes ugly something inside of me; when show destroys substance, and the flash on the surface withers the heart; when love of beauty is really nothing, and inflation of self is everything, — then comes in the solemn charge of Saint Peter.

It is a shame when a man or a society grows so fine outside, and so little and disgraceful within! The Devil has issued a great order, — "Seem to be, and be not," — and the world is obeying it. When we pass through the streets of palaces in a great city, and far more when we see a dignified-looking man or a beautiful woman, the natural feeling is, What noble persons must live in these fine temples! And when we find they are the reverse of noble, that their fine houses or beautiful persons have nobody inside, or worse, then again we hear Saint Peter: "Whose adorning let it not be that outward adorning; . . . but let it be the hidden man of the heart."

Nor do I call a handsome way of living, or the amusements of life, worldly. The full enjoyment of the world and all it furnishes is ours. God "giveth us richly all things to enjoy." Take notice that the generous-minded apostle who said this was himself not a luxurious man:

for Christ's sake he chose to strip himself of all; but not for all that did he proclaim asceticism as the law of life.

As to amusements especially, let me pause a moment upon them. The play of human nature is as much needed as its work. From innocent diversions the heart comes back with new delight to its higher objects. A lower joy, if it is used with moderation, does not destroy a higher joy, but creates a new satisfaction in it. We are made for variety. Besides, we who live in the house of a divine Father ought to know that pleasure in itself is right. I am not bound to show that amusements improve even my health. If I enjoy them, as a bird enjoys its flight, that is enough, so I transgress no law. But add to this that a certain amount of pleasurable excitement is demanded by human nature, and if lacking in purer forms, will be taken in grosser.

The only questions are these: Are our controlling passions those which ought to be the masters; and do they keep the true proportion and order as to the rest? There is a place for them all. It is only the encroachment of one upon another which is an evil. If with us the little has usurped the place of the great, if amusements are our business, they are no longer amusements, — the word means *relief*. If we are beings whose work is to trifle, whose aims are frivolities, our rank is the rank of motes floating in the sun. But no, that were to slander the motes, for their play has business in it. The rule then is, so much play as does not weaken, but invigorates the zest and ability for duty.

Then, as to the quality of our amusements. They are worldly if they are of that sort which discountenances better things. If amusements are such, and so exciting as to make insipid quiet studies, sober duties, gentle affections; if their beauty is of that sort which makes the true beauty of life homely; if your Tyrian purples make the stuff of duty look gray and homespun, then be sure they are worldly and pernicious. I will give then two rules: Not too much; and not of that sort which chills our better tastes.

I am not affected by the usual prejudices on this subject. The prejudices of even good men have swept into indiscriminate condemnation, for example, all dancing, all games, all public shows. How foolish this is, I hardly need to say, and indeed disastrous. "Where virtue is, these are more virtuous." There is a dancing, to be sure, there are games, public shows, most worthy of condemnation. Paris, London, New York, sometimes pour their worst morals on the stage, and husbands, fathers, wives, daughters, sit with open face assisting at these shameless exhibitions.

As to the theatre, permit me to say a few words. The Christian Church is now and always with much unanimity against it, and the world (so called) is with entire unanimity for it. Very rarely has it occurred to them that they both may be wrong. If there is in it a possibility of much innocent and needed pleasure for the human race, nay, of direct and elevating benefit, then it is the duty of the Church to recognize what it might be, and to throw the whole weight of its power against the evils only. It is so great an institution in our life, one which in some shape must stand forever, or as long as man stands, that one would think all men of the Church or of the world would agree to make it such as in some good degree would suit them both, — the Church liberalizing her views and graciously condescending, the world purifying and elevating its taste. It should be under the most watchful care of the best Christian conscience (I mean a conscience wise through liberality), and at the same time under a taste large enough to admit all human interests, but keeping far off from the shadow of ill. All advocates of the drama should know that while it is a fascinating figure, yet it stoops so easily to low tastes in the play, and to low lives in the actors, that to keep it honorable, and a minister of sweet and noble influences, it should be watched with chaste and stern eyes. Any attempt to regenerate this powerful muse should have the sympathy of the Church, — which, however, cannot tolerate it as it stands; its sympathy must be reserved for honest effort to make it as it ought to be. So of all amusements. There is nothing in them of necessity unclean; but as the heart needs the regeneration of Christ, so do all the ways and institutions of man.

In all amusements and in all our life, let not a mad luxury react to a mad asceticism; let us not impose the rule for saints or holy men — and a very questionable rule even for them — upon the young, calling that sin which is no sin, blackening a world already dark enough, and forcing the live human being to become a mummy. Worse still, if a man finds he cannot live the dry life of a mummy, the effect is to drive him either into a hypocritical sensualism or into an open opposition to religion and to his own conscience, while Christ and his pure religion must bear the reproach of it all. "Use this world as not abusing it." The mouth is made for laughter, as well as for speech; everything for use, but nothing for abuse. This is reason; this is religion.

I do not call worldly, a regulated desire for advancement by gain of money, rank, or reputation. These things are natural, and no natural instinct is created to be extirpated, and these instincts are the basis of the order and progress of the world. When, however, a man forfeits the whole of his widely gifted soul to one object, and his eagerness hardens him into steel; when his heart does not soften and sweeten as his fortunes grow; when he does not turn with increasing gratitude and humility to God, with increasing brotherliness and generosity to men, sorry for their failures, prompt to meet their distresses, then be sure the man is worldly.

There is a worldliness, indeed, much deeper than mere enjoyment of the world, and of this few tongues ever speak. I call pre-eminently worldly the men and women who for the sake of the world's good opinion, or of rank in society, sacrifice their better selves, their friends, the truth. Aspirations for good society we must all approve (for our society is one of the highest facts about us); but by good society I mean people with refinements and thoughts, above all, with hearts and with an inward nobleness, for that only is good society; and to sacrifice something to make them friends were wise indeed.

But the sacrifices I speak of are made to reach a very different society. I will not describe it; but whatever it is, at the best it is but a conventional thing. Yet to reach it, or to live in it, many sacrifice themselves, their minds, deserting all true culture; sacrifice their consciences (for to them the rule of fashion is essentially the law of God); sacrifice their hearts, the domestic affections become selfish, greedy, striving (I have seen them poising like hawks in the upper air, looking over land and sea for their objects); become envious, malignant, worshipping what is over their heads, despising what they think under their feet, sacrificing not merely their personal worth, but their peace; for if we except some flashy excitements, nothing can be more unsatisfactory than their lives.

This I call worldly; and I call it worldly also when for the sake of the world people sacrifice their convictions. Zadok was the founder of the great sect of the Pharisees, and he left on record this memorable piece of advice, "Separate not yourselves from the majority," which is the fundamental maxim of human nature in everything worldly. If the whole of our best society were turned Buddhists, how long would the worldly woman or man remain Christian? The usual question is, What will he or she do? Are the best people on that side? And so they snap the most sacred obligations. "They follow still the changes of the moon."

There are several sorts of worldlings; but to sacrifice friends and convictions on a cold and heathen calculation is so extreme, so hateful to God, that I could almost wish you would forget all the rest and think only of this one. There is a so-called worldling of the senses, the man who is his own worst enemy, but he may be kind and true at the bottom of his heart. There is the worldling of vanity, the creature of a silly imagination, a painted little butterfly, — no one can be very harsh with that. But worse than these is the heartless worldling, the man (still more the woman, if it be possible) whose soul has been turned into the cold steel of selfishness; the poised, calculating, systematic worldling, who shows a thousand faces and all frightful, who shines in smiles and is all iron below, who, if fashionable interest beck to him, will set his iron heel on the tenderest heart or the most sacred truth, if it is safe to do so, and at any rate will stand aside to let injury be done; the worldling who is perfect in the let-alone principle, perfect in the cold soul of Cain, saying, "Am I my brother's keeper?"

I sometimes wish there would appear new apostles on the earth to preach common honor, to preach kind hearts, to preach manliness to men and womanliness to women. For, though none of us, I think, can be like the picture I have drawn, yet we are all of us in some degree tainted. It is impossible to stand so near the great ocean of worldliness and not be sprinkled by its spray.

Of the higher and universal form of worldliness I have not spoken at all. I mean that universal exaggeration of the world that now is, — an exaggeration which seems to belong to us as men; the forgetfulness, in the present moment and place, of the invisible, the beyond, the hereafter. We are all of us shut up as in a box, "worshipping and serving the creature," and seeing nothing outside. We are eager and immersed in the thing of a moment, anxious, fretted. Why so intense? Be quiet "The Lord is at hand." In a moment, in the twinkling of an eye, this great scene must be stripped, and we must stand before the face of the Judge, who judges "the deeds done in the body."

Ah, gracious God! make us a little wiser; make us to "live soberly, righteously, and godly, in this present world; looking for that blessed hope, and the glorious appearing of the great God, and our Saviour Jesus Christ." Amen.

www.ingramcontent.com/pod-product-compliance
Lightning Source LLC
Chambersburg PA
CBHW021205230426
43667CB00006B/569